PAUL **MOORE**

THE WORLD'S
MOST
EXTREME
CHALLENGES

B L O O M S B U R Y

LONDON · NEW DELHI · NEW YORK · SYDNEY

Contents

Introduction *6*

THE WORLD'S
MOST
EXTREME
CHALLENGES

For Eva

BLOOMSBURY SPORT
An imprint of Bloomsbury Publishing Plc

50 Bedford Square   1385 Broadway
London   New York
WC1B 3DP   NY 10018
UK   USA

www.bloomsbury.com

BLOOMSBURY and the Diana logo are trademarks
of Bloomsbury Publishing Plc

First published 2015

British Library Cataloguing-in-Publication Data
A catalogue record for this book is available from the
British Library.

Library of Congress Cataloguing-in-Publication data
has been applied for.

ISBN: HB: 978-1-4729-0576-5

2 4 6 8 10 9 7 5 3 1

Designed by Austin Taylor
Printed and bound in China by C&C Offset Printing Co

Bloomsbury Publishing Plc makes every effort to ensure
that the papers used in the manufacture of our books are
natural, recyclable products made from wood grown in well-
managed forests. Our manufacturing processes conform to
the environmental regulations of the country of origin.

To find out more about our authors and books visit
www.bloomsbury.com. Here you will find extracts, author
interviews, details of forthcoming events and the option
to sign up for our newsletters.

Introduction

As human beings, we have always been inclined to test the limits of what we think is possible. It's how we have arrived at the world that we live in today.

Medical, scientific and technological breakthroughs are ongoing, shaping and changing our planet on a daily basis. These developments also affect our knowledge of what is possible in the sporting arena. We understand how our bodies work in ways that were inconceivable just a short time ago. We have technology and equipment that can take us higher, faster and further than ever before. Places that were considered inaccessible less than 50 years ago are now just a few hours' flight away, and we can perform an in-depth recce of them on the internet. In many respects, science and technology have turned the world into a sporting – and adventure – playground.

But while development might have forced the door to this playground open, it is the athletes who play the games. And while we marvel at innovation, it is the human spirit that inspires us. Because it is the human spirit which is willing to put everything on the line simply to see what is possible. It is that spirit that motivates a cyclist to train for days, weeks, months and years in pursuit of the *maillot jaune*. It is that spirit that drives adventurers to keep on trekking across the cold, barren, lonely Polar ice cap. And it is that spirit that motivates somebody to step out of a pressurised capsule deep within the stratosphere simply to see what will happen.

Yes, technology has helped almost all of the athletes featured in the pages of this book in one way or another. But it is the athletes themselves that are willing to challenge the boundaries of what we consider possible. In that way, they are truly exceptional human beings. For every one of them that succeeds, there will be others that do not. The demands of all of these challenges are so great that invariably individuals will fall short in the pursuit of their goal – sometimes disastrously so. Regardless of their success or lack thereof, the simple desire to challenge themselves takes an enormous amount of courage. It is an achievement in itself.

This book is a celebration of courage and willing.

How do you define an 'extreme' challenge? It isn't easy. With endurance and extreme sports booming in popularity, there are always individuals looking to do something 'a bit different' (you usually read about them in whimsical sections in newspapers). These challenges are sometimes whacky, generally pretty extreme, and often demand a physical prowess most people can only marvel at. However, because of limited word counts and a need to draw the line somewhere, we cannot include them all here. So you won't read about people pogo sticking around South America or attempting to do the moonwalk across Ethiopia in the pages of this book.

Rather, the challenges that are included in this book are sporting events or individual pursuits that are so hard or dangerous that only a limited number of people can do them. All of them are repeatable, and as such have pre-defined parameters and measurable outcomes. And, all of them have that wow factor – you know, the one that makes us 'ordinary' people think that these things are surely impossible.

In every way, this list is entirely subjective. What's more, by the time this book is in your hands there is a good chance that someone somewhere will have done something that really does deserve to be included in this exposition of all things extremely challenging (but isn't). That is the nature of profiling the athletes and challenges that push the limits – once one person has done something there is always someone wanting to go a little bit higher, faster or further. There's nothing we can do about that, but if you let us know where we have fallen short, we will badger our publishers and maybe they will let us write a sequel.

In the meantime, we hope you enjoy this exposition of the World's Most Extreme Challenges. It is a testament to what human beings are capable of. These athletes captivate us, they inspire us, and they are some of the few people on this planet who really can make the world sit up and pay attention for all the right reasons. By simply being able to do that, they prove that there really are no limits.

The impact

All of the challenges featured in this book are hard. Very hard, in fact. As a result, athletes have to overcome numerous obstacles when completing them. While these obstacles differ from one challenge to the next, there are a few common barriers to success that many of them share. These are outlined in some detail in the relevant chapters, but to help facilitate an understanding of these obstacles here is a broad overview of the impact of four of the key challenges – heat, cold, altitude and sleep deprivation – on the human body.

Heat

Exercising in the heat has two major impacts on the body: hyperthermia and dehydration.

Hyperthermia has multiple implications for athletic performance. First and foremost, it reduces muscular endurance, and so constricts the body's ability to sustain exercise over multiple hours. It also shifts the metabolism from being in an aerobic to anaerobic state. In this state, the body uses up its carbohydrate stores faster. Finally, it reduces the ability of the heart to pump blood around the body, and so increases the strain on the organ.

Athletic performance in hot conditions can quickly lead to the onset of dehydration. In cases of moderate to severe dehydration, the heart struggles to function normally and athletic performance is impeded. If not remedied, this can be fatal. It is estimated that a human being can last a couple of days without water in hot conditions – although this obviously varies depending on the individual.

Extreme Cold

OUT OF WATER When exposed to cold weather, the body begins to cool. As a result, the ability to sustain a high heart rate decreases, and therefore so does the ability to perform an endurance activity. Because the blood cools in cold temperatures, the VO_2 Max of an athlete decreases. Blood cooling also leads to higher lactate levels in the blood and muscles, further impeding performance.

Athletes performing in cold temperatures are often susceptible to frostbite. Because the body pulls warm blood closer to the vital organs, there is little heat to stop extremities (such as hands and feet) from freezing. Frostnip is the first stage of this and is treatable. If the skin continues to freeze it turns black and becomes very painful it's a sign of advanced frostbite. If the freezing continues, it can affect

the muscles and nerves, requiring amputation.

Dehydration is also a significant consideration for athletes performing in cold weather. The body still loses fluid when exercising in the cold. However, the lower temperatures do not trigger the same thirst response as warm weather activity. Therefore, the body (and the athlete) does not realise it is becoming dehydrated. The result is impaired performance and the possibility of a system shutdown if not remedied.

IN WATER When entering cold water the human body's mammalian dive reflex kicks in. The body adapts by drawing the blood towards the essential organs and thus protecting it against the cold. It does this through a process of heart rate reduction and vasoconstriction (whereby the blood flow is reduced because of a muscular contraction in the blood vessel walls). Hands, arms and legs are the first areas of the body to experience restricted blood flows. However, if the body is exposed to extremely cold water for a prolonged period of time, eventually the brain and the heart will battle for the remaining blood supply – a potentially fatal occurrence.

In 'normal' ocean or river water, acclimatised swimmers can usually perform for a number of hours before their form breaks down. In extremely cold water, this performance is often limited to minutes.

When the body exits the water, this whole process is reversed. The warm blood rushes to the periphery, drawing the cold into the core. Hypothermia is a common by-product of what is a very uncomfortable – and sometimes fatal – physical response.

Altitude

Hypoxia – or inadequate oxygen supplies – can begin to affect an athlete who is not acclimatised above 1,500m (4,900ft). At these heights they may experience an increase in their heart rate and respiration as their Vo2 Max decreases. As the athlete climbs higher, hypoxia can start to have severe physical consequences, such as a pulmonary or cerebral oedema. Initial symptoms of a pulmonary oedema include a tightening of the chest or regular, uncontrolled coughing. If it is not rectified by retreat to lower altitudes, it can be fatal. Cerebral oedemas impact a small number of climbers at higher altitudes. What begins as a headache or loss of clear vision can quickly deteriorate and result in death.

Above 8,000m (26,000ft), climbers enter the 'death zone'. At this height there is insufficient oxygen to sustain human life. As the body deteriorates, this lack of oxygen can impact decision-making and heighten levels of lethargy. It can also cause the vital organs to shut down altogether.

Sleep Deprivation

Different individuals require different amounts of sleep. However, sustained periods of sleep deprivation can have a variety of impacts on the human mind and body. A chronic lack of sleep can have a negative impact on vital organs like the heart, increasing the risk of disease and illness. That said, studies conducted on sleep-deprived endurance athletes have found that their oxygen intake remains stable regardless of the amount of sleep that they have had. However, the athletes perceived that they were working harder than

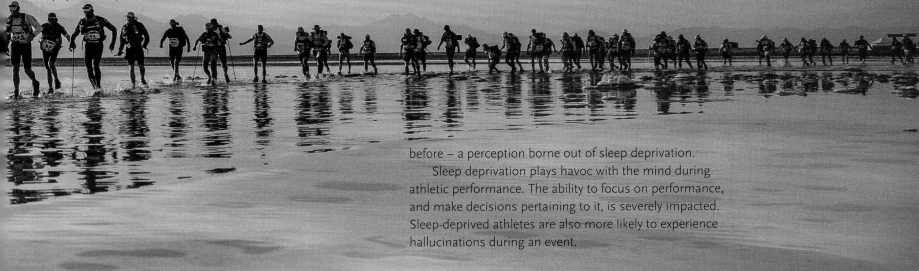

before – a perception borne out of sleep deprivation.

Sleep deprivation plays havoc with the mind during athletic performance. The ability to focus on performance, and make decisions pertaining to it, is severely impacted. Sleep-deprived athletes are also more likely to experience hallucinations during an event.

THE
HIGHEST
HEIGHTS

Type Skydive
Date 14th October 2012
Distance 41,425m (135,908ft)
Main challenges Hostile environment, unknown effects, gravity

Competitors say
When you are standing on top of the world, you don't think of records anymore; all you think is that you want to come back alive.
Felix Baumgartner

ARIZONA · Phoenix · Tucson
NEW MEXICO · Albuquerque
TEXAS · Dallas · Austin · Hous · San Antonio
MEXICO · Chihuahua

A Jump from the Edge of Space

In 1960, Joe Kittinger zipped up his spacesuit, took his seat inside the Excelsior III capsule and watched the balloon inflate. Then he waited. For two hours he looked at the earth disappearing beneath him as the balloon carried him up through the atmosphere towards the edge of space. When his altimeter clicked through 19 miles (31km), Kittinger jumped.

right Joe Kittinger's jump from Excelsior III set a number of skydiving world records that would not be broken for over 50 years

13 minutes and 45 seconds later he was back on solid ground – four minutes and 36 seconds of that had been free fall. The US Government (who were running the expedition) analysed the data, used the information Kittinger gave them to develop escape chutes for high-altitude fighters, and moved on to a different project. But Kittinger had started something – he had set records in almost every skydiving category there was. And records are there to be broken. Over the course of the next 50 years numerous skydivers attempted to better Kittinger's jump. All of them failed.

Then, in 2009, Red Bull announced an ambitious new project: Stratos. Stratos would see one of the world's best BASE jumpers, Felix Baumgartner, carried 24 miles (38km) up into the stratosphere – 5 miles (8km) higher than Kittinger. Once he reached his target height he would jump, free falling back to earth faster than any person had ever travelled before outside of a machine. The whole thing would be broadcast live to the world.

On paper, the plan was relatively simple. In reality, it was anything but.

A team of ex-NASA engineers spent more than three years masterminding the technical aspects of the jump. The balloon they created to carry Baumgartner to the edge of space was one-tenth the thickness of a plastic carrier bag and, when inflated, would reach higher than a 50-storey building. The capsule they designed had to keep Baumgartner alive in the freezing, hostile environment

of the stratosphere. Meanwhile, the suit had to be strong enough to protect Baumgartner during free fall, but flexible enough for him to respond to the many physical demands of the jump.

As might be expected, the first concern the medical crew had about Baumgartner was the threat of hypoxia – commonly referred to as altitude sickness. If everything went to plan, the capsule and the suit would keep him pressurised and so negate its impact on the jump. However, if either the capsule or the suit failed, Baumgartner would struggle with oxygen deficiency which would lead to both physical and mental impairment – in the latter stages of the ascent this would almost certainly be fatal.

The threat of hypoxia was far less concerning than the potential impact of stratospheric pressures on the human body. At 63,000 feet, Baumgartner passed through the Armstrong Line. Beyond this point, the body begins to swell as the gas atoms that bind it together expand and leak. Tissues start to vaporise and the blood begins to boil. Death is not guaranteed (immediately), but prolonged exposure to these conditions is both excruciatingly painful and will undoubtedly be fatal.

Then, of course, there was the jump itself.

Nobody knew the speed at which Baumgartner would fall. What they did know was that, with no atmospheric pressure to restrict it, he would fall fast. After 25 seconds scientists projected that he would be free falling faster than a jumbo jet, and just ten seconds later he would be travelling faster than a speeding bullet (approximately 700mph/1,126kph). After that he would become the first person to pass through the sound barrier – the speed at which an object catches up with its own sound waves. Nobody had ever travelled that fast (outside of a machine) and the impact of passing through the sound barrier on the human body was entirely unknown.

All in all, the risks to Baumgartner were tremendous. And yet, despite his fears (he pulled out of the project for six months during the preparatory phase), Stratos going massively over-budget, and the team missing almost all of their time targets, on 14th October 2012 Felix Baumgartner was cleared for take-off.

After three hours of climbing, Baumgartner reached his jump point.

The footage – and the facts – speak for themselves. After jumping from exactly 38,969.4 metres (24.3 miles), Baumgartner started a 4 minute 22 second free fall that covered 36,402.6 metres (22.1 miles). He experienced 25.2 seconds of weightlessness at the start of his free fall before atmospheric pressures took hold of him. These pressures made his body twist and turn, pushing him into a potentially fatal 'flat spin' – with his head or feet at the centre of rotation. Baumgartner was able to stabilise the spin after

above The balloon that carried Baumgartner was higher than a 50 storey building and made out of high-performance polyethylene that was just 0.0008 inches thick

13 seconds, and from thereon in the dive went to plan.

Needless to say, Baumgartner smashed nearly every single record on his way back to earth. As well as performing the highest skydive ever with the longest vertical free fall (Kittinger still holds the record for the longest time in free fall), Baumgartner reached a maximum speed of 843.6mph (1,357.6 kph) – becoming the first human being to travel faster than the speed of sound.

Throughout the jump the 43-year-old Austrian's vital statistics suggested a general sense of calm. His maximum heartbeat was 185bpm, while it ranged from 155-175 bpm during free fall (and was 169bpm when he hit his top speed). What's more, after examination there were no adverse side effects.

As so often happens, once Baumgartner had raised the bar, it wasn't long before someone else attempted to better his records. On October 24th 2014, computer programmer Alan Eustace claimed the world record for both the highest free fall jump (41,425 metres / 25.74 miles) and the longest free fall (37,617 metres / 23.66 miles). Eustace spent four minutes and 27 seconds in free fall, reaching speeds of 1321kph (822mph). Unlike the fanfare that accompanied Baumgartner's jump, Eustace's self-funded effort only attracted attention once the magnitude of his achievements had been realised.

The physical, mental and logistical challenges of a jump from the edge of space are immense. A quite literal leap of faith, Kittinger, Baumgartner and Eustace helped develop our understanding of human limitations during this highest of jumps – and captivated the watching world in the process.

Felix Baumgartner

ATHLETE PERSPECTIVE

Before the jump I was aware that it's a very hostile world up there – if anything had gone wrong, I might have had only seconds before losing consciousness. I trusted my team, and my skills and training. We had backup systems for everything. But you always wonder if there's something you can't anticipate. Something unexpected. The unknowns can be hard to deal with, and, because nobody had ever broken the sound barrier in free fall before, that was definitely an unknown. However, I also feel that fear is my friend. As long as you can control your fear, it keeps you sharp.

The view was spectacular. I could see the curve of the earth below, but the sky above me was completely black. I'd never seen completely black sky before. That view was unforgettable – and also humbling.

As I stood on the edge I did try to inhale that special moment, but it was all business. It was very important for me to concentrate on what I needed to do. Besides, there was only about 10 minutes of oxygen on my back, so I knew I had to jump without wasting a lot of time. When you are standing on top of the world, you don't think of records anymore; all you think is that you want to come back alive.

It was very different from a normal free fall – in normal skydiving you can feel the air to maneuvre yourself, but the altitude where I jumped is nearly a vacuum. So, with the thin air plus that pressurised suit around me, I really couldn't sense the surrounding environment at first.

We had practised my step-off over and over – I was trained to do what we called a 'bunny hop' off the step to create as little rotation as possible. And my step-off was perfect. But of course I did start spinning eventually, and that was tough. I just kept working on my body position to find a solution that would stop the spin, and once I found a stable position, I never lost it. Still, it was work all the way down. I didn't get to savour the moment until I landed.

One of the cool things about Red Bull Stratos was that this was a scientific flight test program, and we were learning all the time. Personally, I learned skills like how to fly a gas balloon, but I also learned things about myself. As part of my training, for example, the team even did a 'neural mapping' procedure that showed how my brain is wired to work. Plus the results of this mission went far beyond what I learned as an individual. For example, the monitor I wore under my suit documented the first physiological data ever captured from a human falling faster than the speed of sound.

Would I do it again? I think we accomplished our goals. Now it's time for me to move on to the next phase of my life.

For more on Red Bull Stratos, visit www.redbullstratos.com.

Type Mountaineering
Date May – October
Distance from 8,027m (26,335ft) to 8,848m (29,035ft)
Main challenges Altitude, unstable terrain, crevasses

Competitors say
❝The mountain decides whether you climb or not. The art of mountaineering is knowing when to go, when to stay, and when to retreat.❞
Ed Viesturs

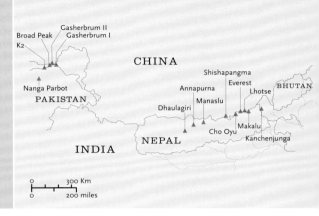

Climb the Eight-Thousanders

To stand on the upper slopes of just one of the Himalaya's fourteen 8,000 (26,250ft) peaks is a remarkable achievement. Summiting the 'easiest' of these deadly mountains takes an exceptional level of fitness, mountaineering ability and pain management. While many are content with 'bagging' a single summit, there is an exceptional group of climbers – 33 of them, to be precise (and counting) – who have stood on the top of every one of the fourteen highest mountains in the world.

right Mount Everest attracts climbers from all over the world

The 8,000m club (as it is commonly known) is made up of an elite group of climbers who have summited, without dispute, the following mountains (listed in descending height order): Everest, K2, Kangchenjunga, Lhotse, Makalu, Cho Oyu, Dhaulagiri I, Manaslu, Nanga Parbat, Annapurna I, Gasherbrum I, Broad Peak, Gasherbrum II and Shishapangma. Although there are additional summits that are higher than 8,000m (26,250ft), they are subsidiary peaks of other, larger mountains. For instance, Mount Everest's South Summit, which stands at 8,749m (28,704ft) – higher than the world's second highest mountain K2 – is not part of the 8,000m club because it is a sub-peak of Everest's main summit (which stands at 8,848m/29,035ft).

Climbing one 8,000m mountain presents unique challenges to the world's best mountaineers. Climbing all 14 of them – four of which make regular appearances in lists of the Top 5 most dangerous mountains in the world – is a truly exceptional feat.

From the moment they leave their base camps, climbers are operating at the extremes. Even Mount Everest, often overlooked as an extreme challenge because of the commercial expeditions that litter its slopes, places enormous demands on a climber. If conditions are perfect throughout an attempt, most climbers can expect around seven days of gruelling ascending and descending to and from the summit. During this time, they will be climbing

across a variety of terrain, including ice and rock cliffs, avalanche-prone snow slopes and wind-ravaged ridges. All the while, they move slowly but steadily towards the 'death zone' – above 8,000m.

On the summit of Mount Everest there is just 33% of the oxygen that is available at sea level. This makes any physical activity exceptionally challenging – climbers who summit these mountains without oxygen have reported taking 15 breaths between each footstep. The lack of oxygen – known as hypoxia – has physical implications and can, in extreme situations, lead to severe altitude sickness, cerebral oedema and death. It can also impair a climber's cognitive functions and cause them to make nonsensical decisions. Climbers have been known to walk off the edges of cliffs or sit on exposed slopes and simply refuse to move (thereby freezing to death). In an environment that punishes the slightest mistake, hypoxia is an ever present danger.

As well as being a considerable physical challenge, the mountains themselves also

pose technical barriers to anyone attempting to climb them. Routes to the summit often cross avalanche-prone slopes or pass beneath hanging glaciers and areas prone to rock fall. Conditions simply worsen when these mountains are buffeted by often unpredictable storms. Hurricane-force winds can bring with them freezing temperatures, whiteouts and massive quantities of snow. Not only can these conditions trap climbers in their tents for multiple days, but they also make ascending and descending incredibly dangerous.

In short, attempting an 8,000 peak is a perilous pursuit. Annapurna I has a staggering fatality rate of 38%; one in four of the people who climb K2 never return to base camp; and both Kangchenjunga and Nanga Parbat have fearsome reputations amongst the climbing community.

Ed Viesturs

I was inspired as a kid when I read *Annapurna* [by Maurice Herzog]. When I graduated from high school I moved to Seattle because of the climbing in that area. I started as a hobby, then started guiding and became more intrigued about going higher and higher. Things went well for me and I thought I had a knack for it. By 1992 I had climbed Everest, Kanchenjunga and K2, and after that I thought: 'I've done three, there's only 11 left'. I thought it would be a tough challenge but it was something I wanted to do, so I committed to it.

To climb an 8,000m mountain you have to want to do it for yourself. You have to be stubborn, patient, willing to endure some discomfort – we call it 'the currency of toil'. You've got to be willing to accept the fact that you aren't always going to succeed. The climbing skills are necessary. When I decided to do it without oxygen, it took it to another level.

It's exponentially harder without oxygen, and the higher you go, the harder it gets. You climb slower and slower as you go higher so you have to be very motivated to keep plugging along hour after hour, knowing that when you get above 8,000 metres there are places where you're breathing 15 times for every step you take. And you know that you will do that for 12 hours. You have people passing you who are climbing with oxygen and they go a lot faster – it's just way harder. I've met people who say 'I'm going to try without oxygen' and you know that they aren't really committed. Once it gets hard and the summit is tempting them, it's like 'I don't care how I get to the top'.

The hardest mountain physically, because of its height, is Everest. It's 29,000 feet and without oxygen you can't compare it to anything else. As a package – the cold, altitude, weather – K2. Objectively, Annapurna; it's one of the most dangerous mountains in the world and you don't choose to climb it unless it's on your list. You can be the best climber in the world and go to Annapurna and still have issues because of the risks you can't control.

When I got to the top of Annapurna I was relieved because I knew that I wouldn't have to go back to it. It was my third attempt and it was scary and treacherous. I wasn't completely relaxed until we stepped off the mountain. That was the moment when I said 'I've done it!' It was like Christmas times one million. It had taken me 18 years to accomplish and it was like a dream come true. I felt very proud. The immediate secondary thought was: 'what do I do now?' It was all-consuming for 18 years and when you have something that consuming and it's gone, you question 'how do I fill that void?'

Ed Viesturs became only the fifth person in history to climb all the eight-thousanders without supplementary oxygen between 1989 and 2005. For more information, visit: www.edviesturs.com.

All of these mountains have claimed the lives of some of the most talented climbers that attempt to summit them.

The first person to join the 8,000m 'club' is widely regarded as being the greatest mountain climber of all time. Reinhold Messner climbed all fourteen 8,000m peaks during a remarkable 16-year period (1970-1986). Indeed, Messner was not only the first person to summit them all, he did so without supplementary oxygen. Since Messner completed his climbs, thirteen of the 33 members of the 8,000m club have followed in his footsteps and foregone supplementary oxygen. In 2013, Korean Kim Chang-ho set the fastest time for summiting the fourteen peaks (7 years, 10 months and 6 days).

Many climbers do not survive a single summit attempt on an 8,000m mountain. To survive fourteen of them is a truly remarkable achievement. It requires a mindset that enables a climber to push on through the many pain barriers that greet them en route to their goal. It demands exceptional technical skills in a hostile environment that punishes mistakes. And it necessitates the ability to 'read' a mountain. To know when it is willing to let you climb it – and survive – and when it is not. Perhaps that is the most remarkable skill of all – a skill that has enabled just 33 people to reach the summits of the world's biggest mountains and live to tell their incredible stories.

Type Wingsuit
Date Year-round
Distance Varies
Main challenges Altitude, gravity, equipment failure

Competitors say
❝Once we got the suits flying, it was then, 'Wow, look at that!' For a few minutes it was like being a bird.❞
Heather Swan

High Altitude Wingsuit Flying

When it comes to climbing mountains or cliff faces, conventional wisdom dictates that the best way of getting back down is to walk (or abseil, in extreme situations). But there is a certain group of individuals who do not abide by conventional wisdom. Rather than walking back down their mountain, they opt for the direct route back to base camp: they jump.

below High mountains are the next frontier in wingsuit flying

Enquiring minds have gazed at the skies for centuries, desperate to emulate the aerial acrobatics of winged creatures. Even the great Leonardo da Vinci produced rudimentary designs of a wingsuit in an effort to understand how human beings could propel themselves through the air.

By the beginning of the 1900s people had a grasp of the principles of flight, but still did not have the materials to do it successfully. Hundreds died trying. The failed attempts – most with catastrophic consequences – continued until, in the early 1990s, Frenchman Patrick de Gayardon finally cracked human flight with his 'bat-suit'. Although de Gayardon died in 1998 in a skydiving accident, wingsuit flying had been born.

Today, wingsuits are made from a variety of materials, although the principles behind them remain broadly the same. The design is based around the shape of the human body. Webbed surfaces form a 'wing' between the arms and the torso and between both legs. As soon as enough air is travelling through the suit, it inflates the membranes around it, keeping it semi-rigid throughout the flight. From that point onwards, it becomes a simple case of physics. Wingsuit fliers generally fall towards the earth at a slower rate than skydivers (60mph/97kph compared to 120mph/193kph), but can travel horizontally much faster (up to 226mph/363kph compared to 60mph/97kph). During a jump, they are able to control their direction and movements to the point where they are able to fly in close proximity to things like cliff faces or through small gaps in the surrounding landscape.

Of course, it is an exceptionally dangerous sport. Injuries are not common amongst wingsuit fliers, but death is (relatively speaking). Travelling at massive speeds with little in the way of protection, wingsuit fliers are constantly on the

edge of control. As knowledge of the sport and the ability
of those who perform it increases, so do the risks. Every year
wingsuit fliers of all abilities are killed during jumps, and it is
generally considered to be the most dangerous sport in the
world.

The quest to push the sport higher and further has
led to some jumps being performed in quite remarkable
circumstances. Some choose to fly off buildings, others
from airplanes, and a small group of fliers head into the
high mountains.

Wingsuit flying in regions like the Himalayas merely
adds to the danger of the sport. Although nobody has
attempted a flight (or BASE jump) off the top of one of
the 8,000m mountains as yet, every year they get higher

and closer to doing so. To be able to 'safely' perform their
jump, wingsuit fliers often spend multiple weeks at altitude
preparing their equipment and planning their flight. During
this time they expose themselves to the perennial threats of
life in the mountains, including: high altitude sickness; the
dangers from the terrain (avalanches, crevasses, etc.); the
threat of being caught in storms; and prolonged exposure
to bitterly cold temperatures.

All of these considerations are part of the build-up to
the jump itself. Wingsuit fliers need calm conditions and
good visibility to perform their leaps. Regardless of weather
predictions, those conditions come at a premium in the high
mountains. If they are fortunate and a 'window' opens, then
they jump.

Aside from the obvious psychological challenge of throwing yourself off a cliff into very thin air, wingsuit flying in the mountains is not easy. Because of the constitution of the air at high altitude, the suits will not perform normally at the beginning of a jump. As such, the initial free fall will be longer, testing the nerves, and meaning that they will be flying in closer proximity to the ground. Once the suit 'inflates', it is a question of maintaining the correct body position while aiming for the landing zone. This landing zone is particularly important in places like the Himalayas, where glaciers contain deep crevasses and rock fields are common.

Needless to say, the number of wingsuit fliers who have successfully jumped from high altitude is small. Australians Glenn Singleman and Heather Swan currently hold the world record for the highest land-based wingsuit flight launch point. In 2006, they performed a jump from Mount Meru at an altitude of 6,604m (21,666ft). Colombian Johnathan Florez executed a non-verified wingsuit jump from 11,358m (37,265ft) in 2012.

Wingsuit flying is, perhaps, the ultimate extreme sport. As exhilarating as it is dangerous, those that are willing to throw themselves off the edges of cliffs and buildings capture the attention and imagination of people around the world. As with any sport, the goal is to keep pushing the limits of what is considered possible. There will be failures – in this sport there always are. But every now and again an individual succeeds, and truly masters the art of flight.

Heather Swan

My husband has been climbing mountains and jumping off them since 1992, when he set the first world record for altitude BASE jumping, and established the fact that it could be done. Before that everyone thought that it was insane. I wanted to spend time with him and do the things that he likes to do. And, you know, if you can climb a mountain and fly off, who wouldn't want to do that?

The climbing is definitely harder than flying. The jumping off is more intimidating, but the climbing is relentless. On Mount Meru, nobody had climbed the side of the mountain that we were climbing. We didn't know the route or what we were going to find. It was exposed, uncertain and those things are stressful over a long period of time – it took us 23 days.

Using a wingsuit in high altitude is different to what you're used to. When you change anything about the way that you jump, it feels wrong and you're not used to it. Jumping into thin air is very different to jumping into the thick air at sea level, or when you jump out of a plane and have forward momentum. At high altitude you're weaker because of the lack of oxygen and you're tired, stressed, and the air is very thin. It takes longer for the suits to inflate so you've got to hold your nerve and make sure you keep your body position so you don't get into trouble. Once they're flying, it's alright.

It's a very surreal experience to stand on the edge of a stunning mountain like Mount Meru and contemplate the fact you are about to jump off it. One part of your mind is completely focused and knows what it is doing, but there's a small part that is shouting 'no!!!' That's the instinctive fear part of the brain. The moment that you step off, time seems to slow down. It's an interesting sensation in that everything seems to be going in slow motion. You see more, feel more and hear more – you just experience more. On that particular big jump the air was thin so at first I thought 'this feels odd'. But I knew that would be the case and we had a plan to dive head down and then as soon as we had enough speed we would pull out and start flying down the Meru glacier. That's what happened.

Once we got the suits flying, it was then 'wow, look at that'. For a few minutes it was like being a bird. Just having that complete freedom and joy – you don't have a care in the world apart from flying your body across a beautiful landscape. You do have time to enjoy it. We weren't proximity flying so we were able to relax and concentrate on flying, and looking, and having the full experience of it all.

I was so relieved and happy when we finished – and totally exhausted. We had been on the mountain for 23 days and hadn't had enough food so we were really skinny. When I opened my parachute, I just thought 'okay, you've just jumped off a 6,000m cliff, now don't land in a crevasse'. The Meru glacier was crevassed, but I managed to land between a couple of them. Then I just concentrated on walking out, and not falling down one. It wasn't over until we were back at landing camp with our team.

Heather Swan and her husband Glenn Singleman hold the world record for the highest BASE jump exit point. For more information, visit: www.baseclimb.com.

Type Climb
Date June – September
Distance 8,611m (28,251ft)
Main obstacles Terrain, altitude, weather

Competitors say
There was one point where I looked up and looked down and thought "whoa, you might have overstepped the line this time".
Chris Jensen Burke

Climb K2

Lying deep in the heart of the Karakoram Range, the forbidding pyramidal faces of K2 reach high above the surrounding peaks. At 8,611m (28,251ft) it is not the world's highest mountain – Mount Everest (8,848m/29,029ft) famously claims that title. It is, however, one of the world's most dangerous, taking the life of twenty per cent of the climbers who attempt to summit it.

below K2 climbs high above the surrounding peaks

During the Great Trigonometric Survey of 1856, British scientists spied a massive mountain deep in the Karakoram Range. Locals did not know the name of it, and so in keeping with the conventions of the Survey they called it K2 (the 'K' standing for Karakoram). The name stuck.

News of this massive mountain sparked interest in the climbing community. In 1902, Oscar Eckenstein led the first serious attempt at the summit but was forced to turn back at 6,525m (21,407ft). Luigi Amedeo, the Duke of Abruzzi, was the next to try in 1909, pioneering a new route along the South Eastern Ridge. Amedeo reached 6,250m (20,510ft) before he, too, was forced to retreat. Eventually it was another Italian, Ardito Desio, who became the first person to stand on the summit of K2 on the 31st July 1954 – almost 100 years after it was first sighted. This remarkable feat of mountaineering would not be repeated for another 23 years.

Today, advances in equipment, Sherpa knowledge and fixed ropes on the harder sections of the climb make K2 far more accessible than it was back in 1954. However, in many ways the challenges – and dangers – that face those who attempt the summit remain the same. There is a reason why K2 has earned the moniker 'the Savage Mountain'.

Climbing high above its surrounding peaks, the topography of the area and K2's northerly position creates a unique recipe for inclement weather. Fierce storms are common, bringing with them whiteouts and winds so strong that they have blown climbers straight off the side of the mountain. These storms often deposit large quantities of fresh, unstable snow, making its steep, pyramidal slopes highly susceptible to avalanches. In fact, the weather on K2 is so severe that it is the only 8,000 metre peak that has not been summited during the winter months.

As well as inclement weather, K2 places enormous technical demands on the climber. Even the most popular

route (via the Abruzzi Spur) poses numerous challenges for those attempting to climb it. Getting to Camp I requires a precarious scramble up a steep glacier littered with the rocks that regularly fall from higher up the mountain. The first major obstacle that greets climbers is the infamous House Chimney – a 30m (100ft) wall of rock. Although most climbers now use fixed ropes attached to it, it is considered a technically challenging climb without them. Beyond House Chimney (and Camp II) is Black Pyramid. Another exposed cliff face, Black Pyramid is a near-vertical 365 metre (1,200ft) mix of rock and unstable ice. It is considered by many to be the most technically and physically demanding section of the entire climb. Beyond the Black Pyramid is Camp III, which sits in an area highly susceptible to avalanches. If climbers make it beyond that point, then they can begin their push for the summit.

Needless to say, the higher up K2 a climber goes, the more dangerous the mountain becomes. At 8,200m (26,900ft), climbers tackle the Bottleneck – an 80-degree snow-covered slope with a hanging glacier immediately above it. Seracs regularly carve off these glaciers and have caused numerous deaths – it played a huge part in the

above Despite fixed ropes, many pitches require technical skills

below Christine Jensen Burke summited K2 in 2014

tragedy that unfolded in 2008 when 11 climbers lost their lives in a single 24-hour period. Beyond the Bottleneck is a stretch of steep, icy slopes leading up to the summit. Horribly exposed, they are the final challenge in what is a truly epic climb.

For those that do make it, there is a brief opportunity to enjoy a spectacular view from the top of the world's second highest peak. But the job is only half done. Descending a mountain like K2 is often more dangerous than climbing it. With fatigue kicking in and gravity pulling them down, it is very easy to make a mistake on the descent. Indeed, one in four of those who summit K2 die on the way back down – a startling statistic that underlines the danger of the challenge.

K2 is known as the mountaineers' mountain. It is a physically demanding, technically challenging peak, and those who have conquered it often refer to relying on skill and luck in equal measure during their climb. Needless to say, not all climbers on K2 get lucky. And in an environment of such savage extremes, bad luck can be fatally punished.

Christine Jensen Burke

For me, K2 has always been an enigma. I knew it was going to be hard, but I didn't appreciate that it was going to be steep from the bottom to the top. That might sound a bit weird, but on Mount Everest there are sections where you can rest – a flat section – but K2 doesn't give you that kind of terrain. If you're not ready for that, it's going to be a big shock.

Aside from the steepness, you have to think the whole way because it really is technical. And much depends on the snow conditions and whether you've got a lot of ice or a lot of rock. You're always having to think and adapt the way that you climb because the terrain keeps changing all of the way up. And just when you think it's going to get easier, it really doesn't.

As a woman climbing K2, people were probably more scared for me than when I've been to any other mountain. Women haven't had a very good history on K2 – the death toll for women climbing was high. So before I went to the mountains, when I told people I was going, I got comments like 'you're not coming back'. I had to confront that before I left.

When you're on the mountain, if you let yourself think negative things, you can put yourself in a frame of mind that really isn't conducive to climbing well and climbing safely. You want to be relaxed and focused. For me, I had to focus on getting up and getting down – one foot in front of the other. If you let your mind wander off onto what could happen, then it could happen because you're not focusing.

There were a couple of times when the going got pretty tough. There was one point where I looked up and looked down and thought 'whoa, you might have overstepped the line this time', and I did wonder for a microsecond whether I would make it down. But my mind immediately switched over to thinking positively that I would get up and get down. And because I had cold damage on my hands from a prior climb I had to be very vigilant of my extremities.

When we looked like we were nearly there, we had a bit of time – maybe an hour – before we reached the summit to look at it and look at the view. Once I get on a summit I give myself a bit of time and then I'm out of there.

On K2 we knew that there was a potential for a whiteout to be coming in the afternoon and I didn't want to be up on the summit very long at all. I could see the cloud below us and all we needed was for it to roll on up the mountain for the whiteout. Anything could go wrong. So I made a point of not hanging around – I like to have a good look and then while the adrenaline is pumping I like to get down.

The view from the top is pretty amazing. We had unbelievable weather – a clear day with low cloud. K2 stands so much on its own and it's so much bigger than any other mountain in the Karakoram region where it sits, so you are looking down on everything. K2 is so independent so it's an amazing feeling. There was a point where I thought 'hey, I'm the highest person in the world at the moment for this tiny moment in time', which is a weird feeling.

Chris Jensen Burke summited K2 in 2014. She is the first New Zealand or Australian woman to climb the seven summits. For more information, visit: www.chrisjensenburke.com.

Type Climb
Date December – February
Distance 141m (463ft)
Main challenges Gravity, ice fall, hypothermia

Competitors say
❝I have very rarely come close to dying in my career – and I did come close.❞
Will Gadd

Edmonton ●
Jasper National Park
Helmcken Falls Lodge
Banff National Park
Calgary ●
Kamloops ●
Vancouver Island
Vancouver ●
Victoria ●
Mt Bakeer-Snoqualmie National Forest

Climb the Helmcken Falls Spray Cave

One of Canada's many spectacular natural wonders, the Helmcken Falls is a 141m (463ft) waterfall nestled deep in the heart of British Columbia. Every summer, tourists flock from around the world to watch in awe as the full force of the Murtle River pours forth from the cliff face. In the winter, it is an entirely different scene – only the determined make it to Helmcken. Most pass by on skis as part of back-country expeditions, but every now and again a group turns up with ice axes, ropes and helmets...

Widely considered to be one of – if not the – toughest mixed climbs in the world, few people are capable of tackling Helmcken Falls in the winter. First completed by Will Gadd and Tim Emmett in 2011, there have been only a handful of successful climbs – and repeats – since the pair finished the route that is now known as Spray On. More recently, Gadd free climbed another route, Overhead Hazard (this time with climbers John Freeman, Sarah Hueniken and Katie Bono) – the hardest route yet climbed in the cave.

Simply making it to the Helmcken Falls spray cave in the winter is hard work. Those hoping to climb it have to wade through waist-deep snow drifts, rappel down a cliff, cross crevasses and avoid the ice-cold waters of the Murtle River. This brutal introduction is just the beginning.

Unlike the surrounding landscape, the Helmcken Falls does not freeze in the winter. Rather, the spray from the falls creates a massive ice cone at its base that can reach as high as 50m (164ft). As the temperature drops, this spray freezes on the undercut, in turn creating icicles. These icicles are massive, fragile, and have a startling propensity to fall without warning. Climbers have to constantly monitor their position in relation to them, as a falling icicle could easily be deadly (even when wearing a helmet).

left To reach the lip climbers have to negotiate a dome-shaped cave

Because of the fragility of the environment, these icicles are much more likely to fall if the temperature in and around the cave creeps above -30°C (-22°F). The severity of the cold is compounded by perpetually wet conditions caused by the spray from the Falls. Everything – from clothing to ropes and axes – becomes coated in a fine layer of ice. This cold, wet environment is not only uncomfortable, but is far from ideal when it comes to executing what is a technically and physically extreme mixed climb.

A mixed climb involves a combination of rock and ice climbing, with ice axes and crampons used on exposed areas of cliff face. These tools allow climbers to tackle pitches that are massively inclined – and at times running horizontal to the ground. To complete the climb (which takes multiple weeks), climbers place bolts in the wall of the cave. This not only enables them to work on various pitches independently, but ensures their safety in the event of a fall. Of course, these bolts can freeze over in the time between attempts, and often have to be located by a climber using a metal detector while hanging from the wall.

The challenges posed by a climb of the Spray Cave are massive and complex. For a start, the cave is enormous. It is also constantly overhanging. The severity of this overhang varies, but there is a large pitch where the wall runs nigh on horizontal to the ground. All the while, the climber is moving across a largely ice-covered surface through a maze of icicles. Some of these icicles can be knocked down, others simply have to be climbed around. If they are able to make it out of the undercut of the waterfall, there is a muscle-sapping vertical climb to relative safety at the top of the Falls. Putting together the entire climb in a single effort takes hours, and on the higher reaches of the wall there is little margin for error.

The dangers of climbing the Helmcken Falls Spray Cave are absolute and omnipresent. From the threat of falling icicles to hypothermia, frostbite and, quite simply, falling off, the odds are massively stacked against success. What's

opposite Every metre of the climb challenges the world's best climbers

right Massive icicles have to be negotiated during the climb

more, if anything does go wrong in this cave, it is almost impossible to execute a rescue. Helicopters (if needed) would struggle to get close to the Falls in the winter, and man-hauling an injured climber up the cliffs that surround the waterfall is almost impossible.

The Helmcken Falls is a place where only the very best climbers in the world belong. It is as hostile as it is spectacular, and from beginning to end poses massive technical and physical challenges to those that climb it. It is, quite simply, climbing in the extreme.

Will Gadd

I was looking for waterfalls on the internet and this one came up. Someone had written: 'That thing is never going to freeze but all this spray ice sticks to the walls behind it and someone crazy like Will Gadd could maybe climb that'. I looked at it, but it's really impossible to get the scale of that place from pictures. I tried to convince a lot of people to go in there and have a look at it, but everybody thought the idea was ludicrous. So in the end, not telling him anything else, I picked a friend of mine up from the airport and said 'We're going ice climbing'.

If you took a domed stadium – the biggest, highest one you can think of – and cut it in half vertically and poured a waterfall 500ft off the lip, that's what the Helmcken Falls looks like. We're climbing up the roof of the stadium towards the waterfall, on the frozen spray of the waterfall.

The most difficult thing about a climb like Helmcken is that it's occurring in pretty much the worst environment I can imagine. It's cold – with temperatures down to -35°C when we climbed it – and there's a lot of water around. So that water either turns to super-cool droplets and freezes on your clothes (turning you into a human icicle), or if it's a little bit warmer, the water doesn't freeze and it starts knocking off some of the really big ice formations and gets really dangerous. So, no matter what temperature it is in there, you have the very worst climbing environment.

The other complicated thing is that you can't just zip out of there. On a normal climb you can rappel down, but on that one because the falling water goes into what we call the 'Cauldron of Death', you can't just slide down a rope back to the ground. You have to slide down one rope and then climb back up to the wall and slide down another. So your normal avenue for retreat is not very good. And there's no way to get rescued there – it would be very complicated. If you get something wrong, the outcomes and consequences are very severe.

We had to really hit it in a different way from other climbs and develop different skills. We had to work out how to operate in that cold, wet environment, how to un-freeze our ropes, how the formations formed and broke off, what happened at different temperatures ... there's a huge amount of knowledge involved in a climb like this.

I wasn't sure I had done it until the very last pitch of the climb. And even then, I wasn't sure until I had pulled over the top of the thing and it was done. There is such a high probability of some little thing going wrong – taking a fall, the wind changing direction – I didn't think about succeeding until I planted both ice axes at the top. Then it would have taken a truck to pull me off. These things are not guaranteed and this one could have gone either way.

That's the hardest mixed climb I'll ever do. I broke my finger and I got such bad shoulder and elbow tendonitis that it took eight months for my body to be functional again. It really took everything to do that climb. I don't want to find another one like it. I have very rarely come close to dying in my career and I did come close – a piece of gear didn't work how it was supposed to and it almost killed me. I don't want to find any more climbs like this. I don't want to see them or hear about them – I'm happy to have done this one ... I'm done!

Will Gadd is a Canadian climber and paraglider. He has pioneered a number of routes at the Helmcken Falls. For more information, visit: www.willgadd.com.

Type Tightrope walk
Date Summer months
Distance Up to 2 miles (3.3km)
Main challenges Gravity, wind, slipping

Competitors say
I once broke both my hands falling from 4 metres ... at that moment I also learned that I could die.
Freddy Nock

Walk the High Wire

People all over the world have been entertained and enthralled by tightrope walkers since the 1700s. At first, these acrobats wowed circus crowds with their death defying exploits performed inside the big ring. But as time – and technology – progressed, tightrope walking changed. Soon performers headed into the great outdoors, and once they were released the challenges they set themselves simply got higher, longer and more dangerous.

There are many different disciplines of tightrope walking. The most common is tight wire walking, which involves a length of wire tensioned between two points. Slack lining has become increasingly popular, where the rope is not tensioned – rather the performer provides that tension. Above an undefined height, performers begin high wire walking, which is essentially a tight wire suspended over a treacherous drop. High wire walkers are the performers that still, to this day, enthral crowds around the world.

Like any elite athlete or performer, the world's best high wire walkers are constantly testing the boundaries of what is possible. Some choose to practise their high wire walks in urban areas, while others attempt to do so in large open spaces. Regardless of where they take place, the performances of these individuals are quite remarkable. American Nik Wallenda completed an un-harnessed 430m (1,410ft) crossing of the Grand Canyon in 2013. At its highest point, Wallenda was 460m (1,509ft) above the Canyon floor. Wallenda is also one of a number of performers who have successfully completed a crossing of the Niagara Falls (high wire pioneer Charles Blondin once did so blindfolded). Some tightrope walkers raise the considerable stakes even higher. In 2011 Swiss-born artist Freddy Nock walked 915m (3,001ft) up a cable car to the top of the Zugspitze mountain with no safety equipment whatsoever – not even a balance bar. Nock went on to complete the highest high wire walk in history – a 610m (2001ft) crossing in China.

While some tightrope walkers choose to wear a harness (or are required to, as in the case of Wallenda's televised crossing of the Niagara Falls), most do so without. This raises the stakes for the walker as a slip or unexpected gust of wind could easily be fatal. Instead of the harness, walkers rely on four pieces of equipment to maintain their balance: the wire, pendulums, their shoes and a balance bar.

Most high wire walkers use steel wires that are up to 5cm (2 inches) wide. It goes without saying that the set-up of a wire that can weigh many tons is not only a massive logistical exercise, but also essential to the safety of the artist. Weighted pendulums are usually attached at specific points along the wire to stop it from twisting during the attempt. Because of the distance of some of these attempts, wires will invariably sag. As such, at the midpoint artists can be

as much as 11 metres (36 feet) lower than the start and end points of the crossing.

There is no standardised shoe for the artists; they wear what they are accustomed to performing in. As such, some will opt for thicker soles, while others choose to perform in thinly soled moccasins that allow them to feel the wire between their toes. Finally there is the balancing pole. Of course, artists sometimes choose to complete a challenge without one. However, the balancing pole – which can be as much as 9m (30ft) long with weights at either end – is crucial for stability. Not only does this pole lower the artists' centre of gravity, but it also helps to increase their rotational inertia (so if they start to move one way, they can use the pole to bring them back to the centre).

Regardless of whether the high wire takes place in a city

left Freddy Nock tackles the Tianmen Mountain Cableway in China

Freddy Nock

I come from a circus family – my father and grandfathers were wire walkers. I started practising at the age of four on the wire. At the age of five I started in the circus with my father. I practised with other things at the circus – horses and elephants – but I always wanted the wire. When I was 11 we started practising the really high wire and I began to have dreams about walking over a lake or walking up a cable car.

When I was 18 I was going up a mountain in the cable car with my mother and I said 'I want to walk up the wire'. She told me: 'it's not possible, it's greasy'. From that moment I started trying different shoes so that I could catch the wire in bad situations. The first time I walked up a cable car was in 1998 – the one my mother told me was not possible. I walked 774 metres, and from then I knew I could do things that other people couldn't.

I don't get scared. I once broke both my hands falling from 4 metres and I said straight away 'I want to go back up again – what happened?' But at that moment I also learned that I could die doing this. It was like someone hit me in the face and said 'if you fall down from this height you won't live'. So I practised. I have a lot of respect for the wire. I know what it can do. I am almost 50 now, but when I am on the wire I feel like I am 20.

When I walked 3.3km at Thunersee on one wire to the ground – with a 1.5 metre swing in the middle – I learned that you control the wire, the wire doesn't control you. I know it can be dangerous. When you make a wrong move with your body you can fall down. So I try to control the wire like I want it to. When I see that I cannot control it I have to catch myself. But this is a lot of practise – how to move the body, how to move the balancing pole.

I did the Zugspitze without a balancing pole, but the conditions were right – there was no wind. I walked for 45 minutes on the wire just holding my hands up. But I had practised and I knew what the wire would do. I was sure I could do it and was sure I could reach the goal.

When I feel really comfortable and have the control of the wire, I look around – and I look down. I did that recently in China when I broke the World Record – 610 metres. I had to look down. My father taught me to always look to the end of the wire. But I have my own technique. I look maybe 1m 20cm in front of me and I can see my foot and the swing of the wire. If big problems come, I can look up and see how the wire is moving towards me. I feel the wire when it comes to me and check myself so I know which move I have to do to hold the balance.

Freddy Nock has broken numerous high wire world records, including the highest high wire walk ever. For more information, visit: www.freddynock.com.

or open space, these poles help to counteract the impact that weather conditions can have on an attempt. All of the world's best high wire artists practise in a variety of conditions to ensure that they are able to deal with variables like strong gusts of wind. To do so, many will train with wind generators that blow at up to 40mph (65kph). However, training conditions are very different to those above a massive drop. What's more, the locations in which high walkers perform invariably mean that dust or moisture attaches itself to the high wire. This simply makes a difficult and dangerous challenge even more precipitous.

Of course, walking the high wire is a dangerous pursuit. Many artists choose to forego safety equipment during their attempts, and every now and again an accident will happen. However, that is part of the attraction of the pursuit. As spectators, we are mesmerised by their ability to perform under extreme pressure. As performers, they are motivated by the challenge of pushing themselves into ever more dangerous situations. It is performance artistry at the extreme.

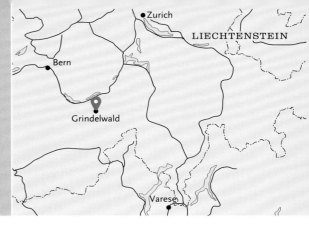

KEY FACTS

Type Climb
Date Year-round
Distance 1,800m (5,905ft)
Main challenges Terrain, weather, gravity

Competitors say
It's a mountain with a psychological advantage over most suitors.
Rob Greenwood

Climb the North Face of the Eiger

Few climbs – few mountains, even – resonate in the populas imagination quite like the north face of the Eiger. In a land of rolling fields and tinkling cowbells, this dark, forbidding wall is something of a freak of nature, and, although often conquered, still poses a significant challenge to the world's best climbers.

right Because of its history, the North Face of the Eiger still has a psychological advantage over many climbers

Buried deep in the heart of the Swiss Alps, the Eiger is an anomaly. Climbing the western flank of this 3,970m (13,025ft) mountain presents little, if any, significant challenge to accomplished mountaineers. But the obsession with the Eiger does not simply come from standing on top of it. Rather, it is with conquering its infamous north face.

The name Eiger was given by local Interlaken monks (meaning ogre), and the north face has captured the imagination of climbers since Charles Barrington first summited the west face of the mountain in 1858. Some 77 years later, Karl Mehringer and Max Sedlmeyer made the first serious attempt at climbing the 'murder wall'. The pair were caught in a five-day storm on the mountain and were found frozen to death at 3,300m (10,826ft) in a place now known as Death Bivouac. They would be the first of many to perish in the treacherous conditions on the north face. Indeed, the history of the Eiger is littered with tragic accounts of the deaths of some of Europe's finest climbers.

Despite the Swiss government briefly imposing a ban on attempts to climb the north face, it was eventually scaled in 1938 by Anderl Heckmair, Ludwig Vörg, Heinrich Harrer and Fritz Kasparek. Harrer's account of this first ascent, *The White Spider*, is one of the most popular mountaineering books of all time.

The route these four men pioneered remains, to this day, the most common way up the north face. The 1938

below The
forbidding North
face of the Eiger
towers above the
surrounding
countryside

route, as it is known, remains an immense physical and technical challenge – despite the presence of fixed ropes on some of the more demanding pitches. Indeed, simply getting to the base of the north face proper requires a taxing climb over steep snow and loose scree. Today, some climbers choose to avoid this initial scramble, and seek permission to take the train to the base of the cliff – the exit known as Stollenloch.

From Stollenloch, the real climbing begins. Almost immediately the Eiger presents climbers with their first barrier: the 20m (65ft) Difficult Crack. This steep pitch of broken rock poses enough of a challenge to dissuade under-qualified climbers from continuing their ascent. For those that are able to negotiate the Difficult Crack, the pitches simply get more technical and physically demanding. The next major obstacle is the Hinterstoisser Traverse – named after the first man to successfully climb the pitch, Andreas Hinterstoisser. In a remarkable feat of climbing that is revered to this day, Hinterstoisser crossed the bare slab of vertical ice and rock in a move that 'opened up' the north face for him and his companions. Unfortunately, the team made the decision to remove the rope Hinterstoisser had secured, and the men were unable to complete their return. All of them died during one of the most harrowing episodes in the history of the mountain.

The challenges keep on coming. World-famous pitches like the Brittle Ledges, Traverse of the Gods, the White Spider and Exit Cracks all pose unique problems for experienced climbers. What's more, conditions on these pitches vary dramatically from year to year. For those launching a multi-day assault on the mountain there are places like Death Bivouac to spend the night. However, in the fading light of

day suitable places for bivvying are often difficult to locate, and climbers are forced to simply find a ledge wide enough to rest on (or dig a seat in the snow). In these instances, there is little to stop them from falling off the face of the mountain other than a couple of carefully placed ice axes and ropes.

The technical challenges of climbing the Eiger are matched by the psychological. The number of excellent climbers who have died on the wall unnerves many of those attempting it. The spectre of past fatalities is combined with the knowledge that a basic mistake can very easily lead to a fatal fall. Stories of climbers falling over a mile with little contact with the cliff face are not exaggerated.

The weather, too, poses a constant threat. These days most climbs take place in the winter, meaning that temperatures on the face can reach as low as -20°C (-4°F). In addition, because of its unique topography, the Eiger can attract fearsome and unpredictable storms that can last for days and, sometimes, weeks. These storms are not only dangerous in their own right, but they can also deposit snow and dislodge ice, creating an even greater threat of avalanches and rock fall.

Because of advances in equipment, climbing the Eiger is more of an athletic challenge than a death-defying one these days (for experienced climbers, anyway). Indeed, while some launch multi-day attempts on the wall, others speed climb it. On the 20th April 2011 Daniel Arnold broke the record for ascending the north face, completing the climb in 2 hours and 28 minutes – a remarkable physical achievement.

The 'murder wall' is perhaps not the out-and-out killer that it used to be. But the north face of the Eiger still presents a formidable physical and psychological challenge for the world's best climbers. Those who tackle it over a number of days often see the Eiger at its best and worst. Those who speed climb it demonstrate remarkable technical abilities coupled with outstanding physical fitness. But all of them know that the Eiger can still bite. And when she does, there is very little preventing a long fall through thin mountain air.

Rob Greenwood

The 1938 route is the classic way to go up. I think about 95% of those who climb the north face do it. Every single bit of it has history. You have places like the Swallow's Nest, the Difficult Crack, the Hinterstoisser Traverse, the White Spider ... every single bit of it has a name because of some fateful piece of history associated with it. It's a rich route in terms of heritage.

You worry about the climb a lot beforehand. But when you start getting onto the route it tends to be fine.

It was big – that was the first thing we noticed. You climb for four hours just on the approach slopes and you've only just got to the Difficult Crack, where the technical part of the climbing begins. So by that point you're about an eighth of the way up and have a lot of tricky climbing above you.

There were a couple of pitches that I remember being more difficult than others. High up, there is something called the Brittle Crack. The north face of the Eiger is covered in this fairly shoddy quality limestone. Throughout the summer months it exfoliates off in big blocks. In winter these blocks are frozen together. However the Brittle Crack can only get so frozen and, yeah, it was pretty hard. You have got to really climb. And because it's so cold – it was about -15°C/-20°C when we were on it – you are using your axes the whole way.

Once you're in the White Spider – which is about three-quarters height – you feel like you're nearly there. But there's still the Quartz Crack and Exit Cracks that are technically difficult, and require a bit of route finding. So it's not over until it's over. Also, you do get freaked out the higher you get. You only really know you've done it when you get out the final Exit Cracks onto the snow slopes.

When we got to the snow slopes it was pretty dark and quite windy. We decided that rather than go straight to the summit that night we would dig a snow cave on the ridge itself. So we dug a tube, basically, to get out of the wind and cold. So the initial 'yay, we're at the top' was marred by the fact we were about to sit down for the following 12 hours, pretty cold and not getting much sleep.

After I got back down I just kept repeating to myself 'Wow, you've just climbed the north face of the Eiger'. It's a sentence you never expect to say.

Even now, today, in this modern age with all of the equipment that we have, it's still a challenge. There are still mountain guides who haven't done it. There are still winter climbers who fear it. It's a mountain with a psychological advantage over most suitors.

Rob Greenwood is a British climber, writer and photographer. For more information visit www.robgreenwoodclimbing.com.

Type Skiing
Date May – September
Distance circa 12.5 miles (20km)
Main challenges Terrain, cold, weather, crevasses

Competitors say
❝When you're skiing on these big mountains, if you fall you're not going to stop for maybe 2,000 vertical metres.❞
Martin Letzter

Ski down Mount Everest

Despite its growing reputation for being a tourist climb, Mount Everest continues to attract mountaineers from around the world. They are lured by the opportunity to stand on the highest point on earth – even for just a few seconds. Most will take their photographs and have a quick look around before beginning the long trek back to Base Camp. One or two, though, do something a bit different. Instead of turning around and walking, they strap on their skis and prepare themselves for an epic descent of this deadly mountain.

right The start of the descent down the world's highest mountain

Since Yuichiro Muira laid the first tracks in the snow above 8,000m (26,000ft), a small number of extreme skiers have pitted their skill (and luck) against the highest mountains on earth. After Muira completed his schuss descent of Everest, there was brief hiatus before the sport of extreme high-altitude skiing really took off. That was largely thanks to the impressive efforts of Italian Hans Kammerlander, who has skied off thirteen of the fourteen 8,000m (26,246ft) mountains. Kammerlander was the first person to ski off the top of Mount Everest, and did so without supplementary oxygen. Seven others have followed in his tracks, but only one has managed to ski the entire way from summit to the base camp without removing his skis. Slovenian Davo Karničar completed this 4 hour 40 minute descent of Everest's South Col in 2000.

Conditions on Mount Everest make any ski descent – regardless of whether or not the skier un-clips at any point – particularly perilous. However, before they have the chance to challenge themselves against the slopes of the mountain, skiers have to summit it. That is no mean feat in itself, even in this day of commercial expeditions.

Climbing Mount Everest is an exceptional physical challenge. The mountain is not considered a particularly technical climb, and there are fixed ropes in place to help climbers negotiate the more difficult sections. But that does not mean that it is easy. Mount Everest is high, it is steep and it is dangerous. Anyone climbing the mountain faces the

opposite The climb up was as challenging as the descent

constant threat of unstable terrain and unpredictable weather conditions. Added to these challenges is the impact that hypoxia (altitude sickness) can have on the human body. To mitigate against its effects, climbers will spend weeks acclimatising to the high altitude. However, regardless of their ability to acclimatise, conditions in the 'death zone' will still take their toll. Oxygen levels at the top of Everest are just 33% of those at sea level. Not only does this make climbing a physically exhausting process, but it can inspire lethargy and enhanced levels of fatigue. Supplementary oxygen helps to combat the effect of this altitude, but does not negate it altogether.

Things don't get much easier for the climbers when they clip into their skis. The lack of oxygen makes the simple act of skiing incredibly difficult. At the very top of the mountain most skiers will manage only a handful of turns before having to pause and catch their breath. Their legs, already fatigued from multiple days of climbing up to the summit, battle for control on Everest's precipitous slopes. This is in no way helped by the condition of the snow and ice on the slopes of the mountain.

The high altitude and inclement weather at the top of Mount Everest create far from ideal skiing conditions. In some years the hard-packed snow can be forgiving. In others it is basically sheet ice. As the descent kicks in the skiers have to carefully select their lines across exposed slopes, through tight couloirs, and along ridges with sheer drops to both their left and right. There are also technical sections of exposed rock and cliff face. Most will choose to un-clip from their skis and rappel down these sections. However, during Karničar's non-stop descent in favourable snow conditions, he opted to ski the steep, technical gullies that ran alongside exposed sections like the Hillary Step rather than un-clip and rappel.

Because of the lines that they follow down the mountain, skiers tend to be forced to tackle parts of Everest that foot expeditions can avoid. As a result, there is a significantly increased risk of avalanches and ice fall along these routes. Should their movements trigger a reaction on the slopes, there is often little stopping the skier from falling many thousands of metres.

It goes without saying that skiing down Mount Everest – or any 8,000m mountain – is a dangerous thing to do. Every year, the mountaineering community is reminded that

Everest can be an unforgiving summit. For those who choose to attempt the descent on skis, that danger is even greater. That is, perhaps, one of the lures of this challenge. The odds are stacked against success in an extreme environment where mistakes are severely punished. Those that do make it back to Base Camp can rest assured that they have tackled the ultimate extreme skiing challenge – and somehow lived to tell their tale.

ATHLETE **PERSPECTIVE**

Martin Letzter

There are two routes: one from the South and one from the North, which we did. They are easy climbs – what climbers would call non-technical climbs where there are no real technical sections. It's basically walking uphill – walking up a really steep slope. But we were skiing this thing. It's difficult to ski things that are steeper than 50-55 degrees, especially at that altitude and depending on the quality of the snow.

You're pretty weak up there. It's not like skiing at normal altitude. You're tired from climbing for so many hours. You can only manage, say, three turns and then you have to stop to hyperventilate for 30 seconds and get your breath back. Then you make another three, four or five turns, depending on how technical the terrain is. Having said that I feel more confident on skis than I do on crampons – I feel more stable. I was a skier first and climber second. I'm still not a good climber.

There are sections of the mountain where you cannot afford to fall – we would call them 'no fall zones'. It's not like the 'hero skiing' that you engage in in North America. When you're skiing on these big mountains, if you fall, you're not going to stop for maybe 2,000 vertical metres. Just to illustrate that, the bindings I had on that expedition were homemade without any form of release mechanism. I didn't need a ski that would release if I fell – I was screwed anyway. And I didn't want something that would release

when I was not expecting it.

There are sections of the mountain that are 55 degrees steep and you have 2,500m drop on one side and maybe a 3,000m drop on the other. You're balancing on a ridge and if you fall you're just going to start accelerating. So you have to ski very conservatively. You're going to make a couple of turns, side step down a metre or two and then make some more turns. You have to be sure not to make mistakes.

I don't think about it in terms of fear, but you definitely have the adrenaline. You need to be a little bit scared to be on top of your game – most athletes perform under pressure. There is a tingling sensation in your stomach and you know that, if you make a mistake, it's going to have real consequences.

You only finish the descent when you are safe. The only time we could be happy about what we had done was when we reached Camp I. We only had 400-500 vertical metres of descent and it was fairly easy. That's when we knew we were safe. You reach the camp, take off the equipment, relax and feel good about what you've done.

Martin Letzter skied off the summit of Mount Everest in 2007 as part of the Se7ensummits project. For more information, visit: www.se7ensummits.com.

Type Climb
Date December - January
Distance 914m (3,000ft)
Main challenges Fatigue, technicality, exposure

Competitors say
'Those nineteen days were such a surreal and intense experience, and I knew it was something I wouldn't repeat in life.'
Tommy Caldwell

Stanislaus National Forest
Stockton
Yosemite National Park
San Francisco
Modesto
Sierra National Forest
San Jose
Merced
Madera

Climbing Dawn Wall, El Capitan

Nineteen days suspended on the side of a giant granite monolith in the middle of a Yosemite Valley winter. That's what it took for Tommy Caldwell and Kevin Jorgeson to finally 'free' Dawn Wall, a route up El Capitan that many expert climbers considered impossible, and that has since been dubbed the world's hardest free climb.

Dawn Wall first captured the imagination of the US media when, in 1970, Warren Harding and Dean Caldwell completed an epic 22-day ascent of El Capitan's toughest climb. Harding and Caldwell aid climbed the wall (meaning that they were assisted by ropes and ladders attached to the cliff face) and famously turned down the offer of a rescue from the National Park Service when a four-day storm swept through Yosemite Valley.

It would be another 35 years before the mainstream media returned to El Capitan – with Dawn Wall once again the focus of their attention. This time, Tommy Caldwell (no relation to Dean) and Kevin Jorgeson were attempting to complete a 'project' that some of the world's best climbers had said was impossible: free climbing this 32-pitch route.

The fundamental difference between free and aid climbing is that climbers only use the natural features of the rock to send (or complete) a pitch (an independent section of the route). Climbers are attached to the cliff face by harnesses and ropes (unlike free soloing, where there is no safety equipment whatsoever), but these are only in place to catch them if they fall. Should that happen, the climber returns to the start of the pitch that they are working on and begins the whole thing again.

Because of the technical and logistical challenges of this project, climbing Dawn Wall took many years

left Dawn Wall has been dubbed the world's hardest big wall free climb

of preparation. Tommy Caldwell first started seriously considering it in 2007, and in the years that followed he examined each of the 32 pitches that individually made up the ascent. During this process he analysed the hand and footholds that would link up the pitches from the bottom to the top of the Wall, and started to attach the protection bolts that he would need to avoid a fatal fall. In 2009, Kevin Jorgeson approached Caldwell about teaming up for the climb, and the pair agreed to tackle Dawn Wall together.

Dawn Wall has been dubbed the world's hardest big wall free climb for good reason. Most extreme multi-pitch climbs have one or two sections that are technically challenging. Dawn Wall has twelve pitches that are graded super expert (5.13 and above on the Yosemite Decimal System), and a further six that are classified as either elite or super elite (5.14 and above). This includes back-to-back pitches rated at 5.14d, the equivalent of some of the hardest single-pitch free climbing ever attempted.

Climbing pitches this hard on El Capitan often involves utilising the millimetres-thick cracks and protrusions on the sheer cliff face for leverage and balance. Under these conditions, Caldwell and Jorgesen were only able to complete manoeuvres on the rock using the tips of their fingers or the edges of the soles of their shoes. If and when they fell, the climbers were caught by safety ropes. However, the lacerations they often sustained to their hands while climbing (and falling) frequently delayed their progress. Indeed, Jorgeson spent ten days of the climb trying to send Pitch 15 – one of the hardest sections on the route. For two of those days he was forced to rest on a portaledge suspended from the cliff face while the cuts that he had received to his hands

healed. During this time, Caldwell – who had completed Pitch 15 before Jorgeson – spent the days working on the technical pitches above, while supporting his partner as he attempted to figure out that part of the Dawn Wall puzzle.

It was a nerve-wracking time, particularly for Caldwell. The pair had chosen to climb in the winter (and often at night) because the route faces south-east, and so sits in the sun for much of the day. As a result, even in winter there is often enough warmth on the wall to affect a climber's grip on the subtle features of the rock. But winter climbing has its drawbacks. As well as being exposed to the cold and wind, there was the constant risk that the weather would turn. Fortunately, Jorgeson was able to send Pitch 15 before that happened, and the pair could continue climbing together.

Indeed, having successfully worked through Pitch 15, Caldwell and Jorgesen needed just four more days to complete the remaining pitches on the route, even though most were still graded as super expert or elite.

Topping out at the summit of El Capitan, the pair were greeted by friends, family and a large throng of media. It was a nigh-on unprecedented gathering for a sport that often chooses to shun the spotlight, but Tommy Caldwell and Kevin Jorgeson had earned it. They had successfully completed a route that many – including some of the world's best climbers – had deemed impossible. They had spent 19 consecutive days perched on the edge of El Capitan's stunning face, figuring out its many puzzles as they worked their way towards the summit. It was not only a supreme physical, mental and logistical achievement, it was a truly exceptional piece of climbing – and the realisation of a dream.

Tommy Caldwell

When the Dawn Wall project began, it was the outgrowth of a ten-year obsession with free climbing on El Capitan. It wasn't like I just walked up to El Cap and decided to free climb it. I had been obsessed by climbing this wall, and the Dawn Wall was the biggest target that I could imagine.

The preparation was the entire process – percentage-wise the ascent was like 0.2% or something like that. Not only was it ten years of becoming intimately familiar with El Cap, it was seven years of searching out the line and analysing it in microscopic detail, then finding the line of holds that link it from the bottom to the top. And then there is the logistical aspects of it; it's a giant puzzle.

The face of El Capitan is an incredible thing. It's humbling and it's beautiful. But living in that environment is hard. You're not walking at all, and you're always exposed to the wind or the sun or the cold. It took a lot of years to figure out how to deal with that stuff. And skin health – we're grabbing these sharp, tiny holds all the time. We build up giant callouses on our fingers that crack and are bleeding. So you have to figure out a way to care for your skin and make it as durable as possible. And if you don't walk for 19 days and you're trying to athletically perform better than you ever have in your life ... there's a lot of elements that go into that.

It was difficult [when Kevin was struggling on Pitch 15]. I thought it was really risky because we were climbing in the middle of winter – we had to do that because of the temperature on the wall. We were incredibly lucky to have the weather that we had and I thought it could change at any moment. But once Kevin started struggling he needed a lot of rest days to let his skin heal. During those rest days he supported me as I climbed through the remainder of the high climbing.

For me, the moment I realised we'd done it – the release of the weight – was still on the Wall. When I got through the hard climbs two-thirds of the way up the Wall I knew I could make it to the end (unless a storm came in or something). That was a magical moment because that was what I had been building up to for seven years. When I got to the top you would think there would have been a huge release, but there was a crazy media event happening; there were 50 reporters on top and there was a live feed. That was distracting to me. I come from a background where climbing is a very intimate relationship between you and the mountain. Having this circus going on – which was partly our own doing – it felt a little strange. But in the middle I had this moment where I finally got through the hard climbing and I knew that this dream that I had been striving for for all of these years was finally going to become a reality – that was amazing.

Tommy Caldwell and Kevin Jorgeson became the first climbers to free climb El Capitan's Dawn Wall in January 2015. For more information visit: www.tommycaldwell.com.

PRO COM

PETITION

Type Bike
Date July
Distance circa 2,125 miles (3,400km)
Main challenges Conditions, terrain, injury, fatigue

Competitors say
The tension of 200 guys riding handlebar to handlebar, shoving, pushing, breaking, almost crashing 100 times ... so many close calls. You're frazzled.
Frankie Andreu

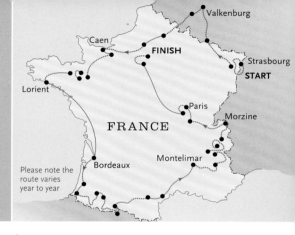

Please note the route varies year to year

The Tour de France

The colourful peloton snaking its way through lavender fields and over mountain passes. The boisterous crowds that line the Alps, the Pyrenees and the Champs-Élysées. The glorious summer days of swashbuckling breakaways and tight bunch sprints. The Tour de France is, for millions of cyclists around the world, the highlight of the sporting calendar. But behind The Tour's glorious – often beautiful – façade, lies is the toughest professional road bike race on the planet.

below Tour de France mountain stages push the world's best to their limits

The Tour de France was borne out of the desire to sell magazines. French journalist Géo Lefèvre, backed by his editor Henri Desgrange, came up with the idea of organising the longest bike race the world had ever seen. The resultant Tour began in 1903, with 60 riders attempting six brutal stages (one of which was 292 miles/471km long). Maurice

Garin was the first of 21 riders to reach the Parisian finish line. Although Garin's win was important, what really mattered was the fact that the race had had the desired effect: boosting the circulation of *L'Auto*. As a result, the Tour de France became an annual event – pausing briefly for two World Wars – and was soon attracting cyclists from around the world.

Today the Tour de France is a different beast from that original race. Instead of five stages, the race plays out over 21, with two rest days added to the schedule. While the route (and distance) varies from year to year, the race averages around 2,125 miles (3,400km). The longest Tour was 3,569 miles (5,745km) in 1926. In addition to the distance covered, the Tour is famous for its climbs. Almost every year the total cumulative elevation gain for the race exceeds 124 miles (200km).

Teams and their riders vie for one of four jerseys on offer. The green jersey is given to the leader of a points competition, with points awarded at checkpoints and stage finishes. Winners of the green jersey are typically sprinters who are capable of hitting speeds of up to 80mph (130kph) on the flat. The polka dot jersey is given to the King of the Mountains – the best climber in the race. The white jersey is awarded to the best young rider (under the age of 25). Then there is the yellow jersey, or *maillot jaune*. The most prestigious jersey in world cycling, it is awarded to the leader of the General Classification – and ultimately the winner of the Tour de France. Yellow jersey winners are exceptional all-round athletes who are tactically astute and able to compete both on the flat and in the mountains – they are the masters of their sport.

With between 20 and 22 teams vying for one of these jerseys, the competition is intense. Each of the nine riders selected by a team for the race has a specific role to play. Every team has a leader, who is ultimately expected to produce the results. That leader is supported by a group of domestiques. The role of these eight men is, by and large, to ensure that their team leader is able to achieve his objective in the race. As such, domestiques cover everything, from collecting nutrition and hydration to pacing riders through the phases of a Stage, responding to attacks from rivals, and occasionally going for individual glory (if that doesn't compromise the overall ambition of their team).

The pressure to deliver results means that some riders are willing to compete with severe injuries and even broken bones. These are the visible scars of the Tour – the race can inflict wounds that run much deeper. The Tour is a gruelling competition that places each and every rider under enormous mental and physical strain. Regardless of the stage and incidents on it, riders have to finish every stage

below One of the defining images of a European sporting summer

within a (variable) time limit set by the organisers. On the early flat stages this is often straightforward for uninjured riders. But as the days wear on and the fatigue, injuries and mountains kick in, every year many are forced to withdraw.

The drama and demands of the Tour de France have made legends out of the likes of Bernard Hinault, Eddy Merckx, Miguel Indurain and Jacques Anquetil. Unfortunately, both the prestige and the demands of the race mean that doping has dogged the sport for decades. In 2012, Lance Armstrong was one of the athletes implicated in a report citing widespread doping violations by members of the US Postal Team. Armstrong was subsequently stripped of his Tour results – including his seven yellow jerseys.

There are few annual professional sporting events that capture the popular imagination like the Tour de France. It is a race that pushes the world's best cyclists to the very limits of their physical and mental endurance – and quite often beyond. In so doing it shines a spotlight on what human beings are capable of achieving – and how far some are willing to push themselves in pursuit of the ultimate prize.

Frankie Andreu

It's the largest cycling sport event in the world and the entire world is focused on it. And it's a grand stage that can make or break a rider's career. Everybody who turns professional, as they move up the ranks, is trying to get a selection to ride the Tour. It's the best riders in the world competing with each other day after day for 21 days straight.

There's a ton of pressure because you've made a nine man selection, so you're taking away from some of your other teammates who wanted the Tour. But just being there against the best guys – the team expects results. You have internal pressure because you want to do well; you want to win a stage or be in the breaks. So it's a lot of pressure every single day – you pretty much don't get a day off. The only time you might is if you're a sprinter and you're going into the mountains, then you don't have to perform (but you still have to get through). And if you're a climber on a sprinting stage, you don't have to perform, but you need to stay out of trouble, stay in front and not lose time. So there's never a day off.

That first week, the nervous tension saps you. It could be dead flat, but at the end of the day you could be wrecked. The tension of 200 guys riding handlebar to handlebar, shoving, pushing, breaking, almost crashing 100 times ... so many close calls. You're frazzled. And on top of all that there's the physical demands of going 40mph, flying around corners trying to get to a finish. That's the first week. After that you're into the second and third week and it's the demands of racing and getting over mountains.

It's super important that you eat and drink correctly. The thing is, you're not eating for that day. You're eating for two or three days down the road. You're trying to keep your reserves up. Because the moment you bonk, run out of energy or out of reserves, you can't dig any more. You can't suffer. That's when you get dropped and can't finish – and can't get any results.

If you crash, it's one of the only sports where they pick you up, put you on your bike and you keep going. I remember one year in Holland I crashed on the first day and ripped open my body. The body takes a lot of extra energy to heal itself, on top of trying to compete in the Tour. So when you see these guys who are all torn up, it's almost like they're doing double work – trying to recover and be able to compete.

There were times when I had to do a bunch of work. There was one stage where I got dropped with 100km of racing to go with two big mountain passes left to cross. I remember getting to the end and not being able to speak and then getting to the hotel and not being able to get in the shower. I lay on my bed for 45 minutes recovering just to get my shoes off so I could get in the shower.

I finished nine tours. Coming down the Champs-Élysées and seeing the Eiffel Tower while knowing you managed to get through three weeks and finish the Tour ... I always had shivers and tingles up and down my spine. I almost won in Paris in 1996 – I got second. I was so close to having a career-making Stage win, but I had it ripped away from me.

Frankie Andreu completed nine Tour de France (1992-2000). For more information, visit: www.frankieandreu.com.

Type Dive
Date Year-round
Distance Varies (dependent on discipline)
Main challenges Drowning, adverse physical response

Competitors say
The deeper you go the more dangerous it is.
Herbert Nitsch

The Deepest Freedive

Most people have been freediving. A literal interpretation of the sport involves simply swimming beneath the surface of the water while holding your breath. But true freedivers do something a little different. They challenge the depths of the ocean in a bid to explore the 'big blue' – and their own physical limits.

right Herbert Nitsch spent hundreds and thousands of dollars perfecting his sled

The human body is a remarkable thing. When exposed to extremes of heat or cold, it regulates its own blood flow to ensure that essential organs continue to function. It does the same when exposed to water. Almost as soon as a person's face is immersed in cold water the mammalian dive reflex kicks in. This reflex triggers an immediate contraction of the blood vessels, keeping blood close to the essential organs. The heart slows down and there is a reduction in the residual volume of the lungs, so much so that under normal circumstances the ribcage would explode. But it doesn't. Because at the same time the blood vessels inside the lungs swell up with blood and that compensates for the loss of volume due to the pressure. Meanwhile, the spleen contracts, which releases more red blood cells into circulation and non-essential processes – like digestion – slow down or stop. This all happens without you even noticing.

The greater the depth, the greater the adaptation of the body. At extreme depths the lungs are able to compress to the size of a fist, and the heart can slow down to just 20 beats per minute. With a controlled return to the surface the body is able to reconfigure itself and within minutes of exiting the water (usually) functions normally again.

As with any sport freedivers are constantly challenging the limits of what they are capable of – and what many people think is possible. The sport is split into eight major disciplines that vary depending on the type of equipment that is used during the dive. No Limits is the category that is grabs the majority of the headlines.

No Limits divers risk everything in the pursuit of the

opposite The key to a successful freedive is complete focus

greatest depths possible. Usually using a sled to descend and an inflatable ballast to return to the surface, divers are able to go down hundreds of metres. In 2007, Austrian freediver Herbert Nitsch set a recognised world record for the deepest dive ever recorded: 214m (702ft) in Spetses, Greece. In 2012, Nitsch bettered that record, but passed out on the surface after reaching 253.2m (830.8ft).

Because of the depths that they reach, the pressure on – and importance of – the machinery involved in a dive is immense. No Limits divers can spend hundreds of thousands of dollars trying to improve the performance of their equipment, and so the safety of their dives. However, the history of No Limits freediving is littered with tragic stories of divers who never made it back to the surface – often because of equipment failure. Perhaps the most high-profile death was that of Audrey Mastre, a world-record freediver who was killed when the ballast that was supposed to help her ascend failed after she had reached a depth of 171m (560ft).

No Limits diving is just one of the many sub-divisions of freediving. At the other end of the equipment spectrum is a category favoured by purists: Constant Weight Without Fins. In this category, the freediver descends and ascends using only their own muscle strength (No Limits divers are often exceptional freedivers in this category as well). Considered the 'purest' form of freediving, this discipline requires the diver to be able to perfectly coordinate their physical exertion with their breath management and equalisation. William Trubridge holds the record for the deepest dive in this category, reaching 101m (330ft) in 2010.

Regardless of the category in which they compete, freedivers who push the boundaries and break world records are in exceptional physical shape. Much of their strength work is based around the core muscle groups, and many train using a combination of pilates and yoga. The latter is particularly important as it helps channel another essential element of freediving: the mind. Many freedivers will meditate before a dive, trying to instil absolute calm and shut off thought processes before going under. Thoughts and brainwaves take energy, which requires oxygen, and so the freediver who can shut these off is able to stay under for longer and so go deeper.

Freediving is as much a mental challenge as it is physical. In challenging themselves to reach the depths of the ocean, freedivers explore the boundaries of what is physically possible.

Herbert Nitsch

One time the airlines lost my luggage on the way to a diving safari and I was forced to take some pictures with a snorkel. A friend asked 'how deep can you go?' because he was amazed by my performance. That's when I started freediving.

From the physiological point of view, you don't feel the pressure on your extremities – your legs, arms and things. You only feel it on the empty spaces – like the lungs, sinuses and ears. The sinuses and ears you can equalise, but the lungs you have to train to deal with the pressure. Now more and more people get squeezes in the lungs because they cannot take the pressure and the vacuum inside the lung causes a rupture of blood vessels. In mild cases you spit blood, in extreme cases you experience oxygen saturation for a couple of days. In very bad cases – there has only been one – it is fatal.

I started a bit late with No Limits. I did all of the other disciplines. But the reason I started late was because I couldn't equalise. But then I found a different technique for equalising.

The other reason I didn't start earlier was because I didn't think that the other competitor's sleds were safe. There was no reliable back-up. The system my competitors had was very prone to failures, and I didn't see a way to make it safe enough. Then I found a way. The last dive that I did, if I had done it with any other sled, I wouldn't be talking to you. I would be dead for sure. In the end, the automatic systems of my sled saved my life.

It cannot be frightening when you dive, because any form of anxiety or adrenaline – or even excitement – causes the consumption of oxygen. That means that you have to be in a calm state both mentally and physically.

But being mentally and physically calm is not the same thing. And that's probably one of the hardest parts of freediving: staying calm. Whatever discipline you're doing, you have eyes looking at you – safety divers, the media, cameras – and you have to start at a certain time. But at the same time you have to be calm as if you're waking up on a Sunday morning. You have to achieve that state. If you are even a little bit excited, then you are using oxygen and you shouldn't start because you won't make it.

It is hard to say if there is a specific limit on how deep humans can go. It depends a lot on how much risk you are willing to take. Everyone sees risk differently – and there are concerns over risk management. The costs of covering risks are substantial – my last attempt cost me $250,000. Where did that money go? Safety. If I invested more, it would have been even safer.

The deeper you go the more dangerous it is. Of course, you can reduce the danger by safety mechanisms, but there is always risk involved. My goal was – or is – 1,000ft and I am sure that it is doable and manageable from a safety point of view. But to make it safe involves a lot of logistics. The limit might be deeper than 1,000ft – maybe quite a lot deeper – but it will be more and more risky.

Herbert Nitsch is an Austrian freediver who has held records in multiple disciplines, including the deepest diver ever recorded. For more information, visit: www.herbertnitsch.com.

Type Airplane
Date Year-round
Distance Up to 3.7 miles (6km)
Main challenges G-Force, wind, crashing

Competitors say
You need to be at one with a machine to the degree where you don't think about what you are doing with it.
Nigel Lamb

The Red Bull Air Race

'Those magnificent men (and women) in their flying machines, they go up tiddly up up, they go down tiddly down down ...' Crowds have been enthralled by the aerial acrobatics of pilots ever since the Wright Brothers invented their 'flying machine'. But few pilots in history have performed on a stage as demanding or as popular as the Red Bull Air Race.

below Pilots negotiate a course marked out by inflatable pylons

Launched in 2003 by Austrian drinks manufacturer Red Bull, the Air Race is designed to test the skills of the world's best stunt pilots. The concept is relatively simple: pilots would record a series of timed laps around aerial obstacle courses across the world. Although the competition began with only a handful of events in 2003 and 2004, the formalised race series really took off in 2005. From that point onwards it grew in popularity until, in 2009, Red Bull made the decision to postpone it pending a re-organisation. A three year hiatus followed, before the Series was re-commenced in 2014.

Although there have been a few tweaks and changes to the rules and regulations around the re-launched series, the fundamentals of it remain the same. At each event the pilots in two classes (Master and Challenger) take part in training runs, followed by a qualification run. Following qualifying, pilots are pitted against one another in a Top 12 run, with the six winners and two fastest losers advancing to the Super 8. From the Super 8 to the Final 4, pilots then battle it out for positions on the podium. Much like motor racing series around the world, points are awarded after each event, with the pilot who has accumulated the most number of points being awarded the World Championship title.

Because the series takes place in a variety of countries, the setting for each of the courses changes accordingly. As a result, so do the demands placed on the pilots. The courses tend to be 3.1 miles (5km) long, although some extend over 3.7 miles (6km). Pilots race between a series of 25m (82ft) inflatable pylons placed around the track. There are penalties for hitting these pylons (which are designed to disintegrate in a collision) or flying too high through them. Other than that, it's down to the pilot to find the fastest line through the course.

This is far from easy. Unlike conventional motor racing,

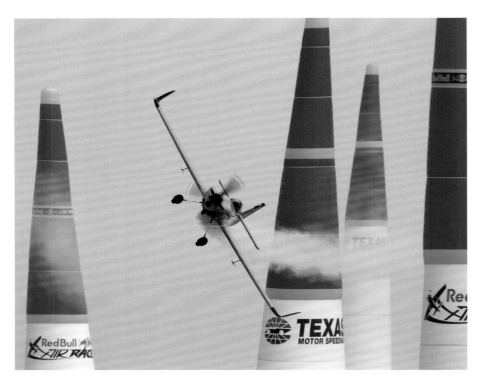

Red Bull Air Race pilots are effectively racing in three-dimensions. What this means is that pilots are not only tracking left and right during a lap, but up and down too. The level of competition and the speed at which these pilots fly means that any misjudgement on altitude or direction can have a significant impact on their final standings. What's more, during a run pilots will have to contend with external variables like wind strength and collisions with passing birds, both of which can have a significant – and detrimental – impact on their times.

Speed is everything in this race. The stunt planes certified for racing are small and light to maximise their manoeuvrability. The fastest plane, the Corvus Racer 540, has a top speed of 273mph (440kph) – significantly faster than a Formula One car. Flying at these speeds on tight, technical courses places an enormous amount of g-force on the body of the pilot. The planes are capable of pulling into a vertical orientation faster than a fighter jet. In so doing, pilots withstand up to 12g of force – the equivalent of twelve times the pilot's body weight being pushed down on top of

below The air race course is 3D – left, right, up and down

them. Internally, high g-forces push blood towards the legs and make it hard for the heart to pump back up to the brain. As a result pilots can quickly find their vision impaired or, in extreme cases, experience a brief loss of consciousness. To combat this, pilots tense their muscles in an effort to force the blood back towards their heads. It goes without saying that any loss of consciousness during a flight can be disasterous.

To maximise their speed through the course, pilots will also perform barrel rolls and steep, banked turns. Again, the g-force (both positive and negative) that these manoeuvres place on the body requires physical management. What's

more, many of these manoeuvres take place just metres off the ground, leaving little room for any errors of judgment.

The fact that only one plane has crashed (non-fatally) during the many years of the Red Bull Air Race is testament to the skill of the pilots involved in it. These pilots are able to withstand considerable g-forces while racing their planes through tight, technical courses. They travel faster than any other competitive motor racers, and they do so in an ever-changing, uncontrollable environment. In short, they push their planes – and their bodies – to the limits of what is possible.

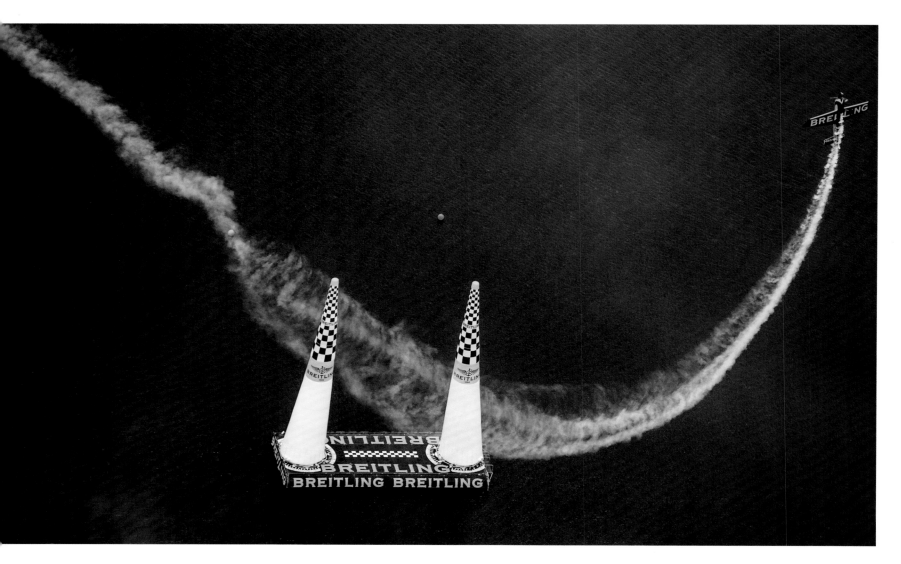

Nigel Lamb

The most important thing from a physical standpoint is that you need to be at one with a machine to the degree where you don't think about what you are doing with it. You've strapped wings on your back, basically. From the point of view of the forces on your body, you get very used to the g-force, which is one of the most crucial things to be at home with. It is unlike wheeled sport – which has lateral forces. You have to get used to that and be able to combat that mostly by using reflex, otherwise you use up all of your brain space, which you need for precision. The rolling forces are also very hard on your neck. These airplanes roll at over 400 degrees per second and we use full control deflection so it really throws your head around and you need to have that under control.

We've all done thousands of hours of training. I'm never thinking 'I must press harder with my left foot because yesterday when I did this the nose veered'. I don't think about my hands and feet at all. I just think about strategy: having the right speed in the start gate, where is the wind coming from?

The biggest difference between wheeled sports and what we do is that we have a two-dimensional track marked on the ground but we fly in three dimensions. You might not be correct in your assumption of where the perfect racing line is for the given wind because it is invisible. But you have to have a mind picture of where it is. You're thinking only of taking your body down that line and going as close as you can to the air gates to get the shortest possible line and go the fastest you can and make the least mistakes so you can win. You're thinking of the big picture – not the details.

You need to be in the position where you and your machine never arrive at any point on the track without your brain having been there a couple of seconds before. You don't want your brain to get there five seconds before because then you will start making mistakes as you are thinking too far ahead. It's a trick to be able to prepare to do that.

On the track I've never frightened myself. I feel incredibly comfortable – you are the master of your destiny. We're like slalom skiers. You should never get into the situation where you are skidding somewhere and going to hit something; the only thing you will hit is the ground (which you need really to avoid). You have to be comfortable enough with your own limitations and those of the machine so that you don't hit the ground. If the situation is really not good, you always have the option to climb out of the track.

Sometimes you think you've put together the perfect lap and then you get the time and find out you didn't. You have to think that you know where the right line is but it changes. If the wind changes in direction or strength, it changes the track or the corners. So you can be in a situation where you come out and you think 'that was awesome', but then you come out and you see that you were a second slower. You made a mistake that you didn't know about. But it is a fantastic feeling when you put together a really good lap and it turns out that nobody beat you. That's awesome.

Nigel Lamb is a Master Class pilot in the Red Bull Air Race World Championship. For more information, visit: www.nigellamb.com.

Type Swim
Date February
Distance 54.6 miles (88km)
Main obstacles Competition, injury

Competitors say
After I finished... I had pain in every area of my body. I will never forget that feeling.
Petar Stoychev

Maratón Acuático Internacional Hernandárias-Paraná

Every February – conditions permitting – the Paraná River plays host to the world's longest, single-stage professional swimming race. Following the 54.6 mile (88km) course from the town of Hernandárias to Paraná, the world's best marathon swimmers compete for up to 10 hours in a bid to claim a coveted professional title.

At 9:00am on 21st February 1965, eleven swimmers took to the waters of the Paraná River in the town of Hernandárias, Argentina. Their goal lay 54.6 miles (88km) away: the city of Paraná. For the rest of that day those athletes swam shoulder-to-shoulder, battling for the win. In the end, the race was declared a draw, with local hero Horacio Iglesias and Egyptian Abou Heiff crossing the line in a time of 10 hours 31 minutes and 41 seconds. The race was repeated in 1966, and then suspended for 27 years before eventually returning to the marathon swimming calendar in 1993. Since then the Maratón Acuático Internacional Hernandárias-Paraná has been a near-permanent fixture on the FINA Open Water Swimming Grand Prix circuit.

A single-stage point-to-point swim, the race follows the winding course of the Paraná River through the Argentinian countryside. Swimming downstream, competitors can reach speeds of up to 6.1mph (9.9kph) or 2.7 metres per second. While the current is certainly an assist to the swimmers, conditions in and on the river can be anything but. Because of the topography of the region, strong winds and heavy rainfall often make water conditions hazardous, and have led to the cancellation of a number of swims since 1993 (most recently in 2012). In the years that the swim does go ahead, conditions in the water are challenging. Visibility is poor, and athletes are forced to contend with waves of up to a metre (3ft) high, as well as the inevitable flotsam and jetsam that accompanies competition in busy, urban waterways.

Because of its affiliation with FINA, rules around the race are strict. Swimmers are allowed to wear approved swimsuits, goggles, a maximum of two swim caps, nose clips and earplugs. That is all. Although water temperatures in the Paraná River are relatively warm (usually around 28°C/82°F), swimmers are allowed to use grease or fat to help them retain body heat. They are, after all, competing in that water for up to 10 hours. Aside from feeding at pre-defined swim platforms, once the race is underway the athletes are allowed no outside assistance. As such, it is down to the swimmer alone to determine their pace, positioning and tactics during the course of the race.

Because of the quality of the field attracted to Hernandárias-Paraná, the competition is fierce. Open water swimming is a notoriously aggressive sport. Like cyclists, swimmers gain benefits from slipstreaming (or 'drafting') behind one another. As such, in races like Hernandárias-Paraná they will swim in a tight group, with athletes battling for a place 'on the toes' of their competitors. This is particularly the case in a race like this, where following the fastest currents can make an enormous difference. Positioning is everything and with up to 25 athletes competing for the best route in the water, swimmers regularly come into contact with one another. Punching and kicking (not deliberate ... most of the time) is common in the pack, while some swimmers are forced into the shallow waters or out into the slower currents. Like cyclists, if these

swimmers get dropped by the pack, it is often impossible for them to catch up again. In these instances, they face a long, lonely swim to Paraná.

It goes without saying that the physical strain of a single-stage swim like Hernandárias-Paraná is immense. Completing a 54.6 mile (88km) swim is a huge undertaking in its own right. To do so against the world's best swimmers

merely adds to the level of physical strain. Every year swimmers are forced to retire through exhaustion or injury (most commonly shoulder strains). Fuelling also plays a role, with athletes often struggling to retain their nutrition and hydration in the melee of the race, not to mention the dirty, choppy waters of the river. Those that do complete the race are the ones that are able to manage the pain that is part

above Variable river conditions mean that organisers cannot hold the race every year

and parcel of professional marathon swimming.

Despite the distance of the race, the finish can often be very close. In 2013 Luciano Sales Rubio secured the win in 9 hours 39 minutes and 42 seconds. Damian Blaum was less than a second behind him, with Saleh Mohammad a further second back. That said, there are years when a breakaway is successful. In 2009, Damian Blaum made his move 6 hours into the race to establish a lead of over a kilometre – enough to secure a comfortable win.

Swimming 88km is a considerable physical challenge, and to do so in a competitive, single-stage race is immense. Marathon swimming is a fast, unforgiving sport. It pushes some of the world's fittest athletes to their physical and mental limits over a period of hours. As the longest event of its type on the calendar, the Maratón Acuático Internacional Hernandárias-Paraná is a true test of physical and mental strength. It is a test that few will ever experience, and fewer still will pass.

Petar Stoychev

The race starts early in the morning – around 7 a.m. – and it takes around 10 hours depending on the level of the river. It's a really prestigious event to complete – the longest race in the world.

You must be really prepared for the race; you can't just go and swim it. You need to be ready because racing under the Argentinian sun and swimming in the River Parana for 10 hours in the brown/yellow water – it's not easy. The water is between 24-26°C, you don't have much visibility. It's a very tough race, and it's challenging for all the marathon swimmers to do it. It's a prestigious competition too, and once you have it in your career you believe much more in yourself.

The strategy is very important in the race, and the coach is very important – the person in the boat. It is very important to be in the fast current. If you are not in a good position with the good current, you have no chance to get a good result. So the strategy is to have a really good navigator with a good guide who can put you in the best position for the race. If you go on the side where the current is not strongest, you will definitely lose the speed and the pack – it is everything.

The difficulty is also that the boats, which follow the swimmers, are rowing boats by tradition. It's more difficult to follow the rowing boat, because it's more difficult to manoeuvre that boat in the current.

It was my first race in my marathon career, and my first race in the World Cup Series. After I finished (I think in eighth place), it was very painful for me for the next couple of days. I had pain in every area of my body. I could not sleep in any position the night after the race; everywhere was hurting. It was very painful and

I will never forget that feeling.

The winner is a very strong swimmer. They are able to prepare for a tough event. Physically they are very good; they have really good endurance. They are stronger than the pain and, you know, to be alone and to swim for 10 hours ... that is not easy.

When you finish, you feel very satisfied. This is another stage of your career. So when you finish you think 'I did it'. You have finished the longest race in the series – you can only be proud of yourself.

Petar Stoychev won the Maratón Acuático Internacional Hernandárias-Paraná in 2005. For more information, visit: www.petarstoychev.com.

Type Bike
Date May – September
Distance Varies
Main challenges Competition, injury, form

Competitors say
❝I definitely think it can be done, but not just because you're the strongest rider – everything else has to go in your favour.❞
Stephen Roche

Win the Triple Crown of Cycling

Winning a Grand Tour is the pinnacle of many cyclists' career. However, the very best in the world aspire to more. The greats will aim to demonstrate their versatility with wins at all three Grand Tours during their careers (nobody has achieved this in a single season). The strongest will try to win two Tours in a single year – something only eight men have managed to do. Then there are those that aim to go one better, and claim the 'Triple Crown of Cycling'.

To complete the Triple Crown of Cycling, a cyclist has to win two Grand Tours (historically the Giro d'Italia and Tour de France) and the Road World Cycling Championships in a single season. In so doing, they unite the maglia rosa (Giro), maillot jeune (Tour) and the rainbow jersey worn by the UCL world champion. Two cyclists have managed to achieve the feat: Eddy Merckx (1974) and Stephen Roche (1987). Miguel Indurain came close to joining this elite club, winning the Tour and the Giro in 1993 but finished second at the Worlds.

Beating the world's best cyclists over three of the biggest races in a single season is a formidable achievement. Grand Tours are pressure-cooker events, particularly for the team leaders who are all expected to pick up stage wins and post strong general classification performances. To help them do so, the strongest teams will attempt to dictate the peloton, exploiting weaknesses in the competition while playing to the strengths of their own leader. The winning rider is the one who is able to attack when the opportunity arises, and defend when they themselves are being attacked. In this respect, it is not only a test of physical strength, but it is also a mentally exhausting, tactical battle. Because of the relentless pressure, most professional riders will aim to peak for a single, specific Grand Tour during the season.

Any attempt at the Triple Crown begins at the Giro d'Italia. A 23-day stage race predominantly held around Italy, the Giro is famous for its challenging Alpine climbs, occasional bouts of inclement late-spring weather, and the passion of the Italian *tifosi*. The pressure on Italian riders is immense, with the fans (and their teams) desperate for local riders to secure the maglia rosa. During his Triple Crown year, Stephen Roche earned the ire of the *tifosi* when he disobeyed team orders and beat team leader Roberto Visentini to the overall victory. His win at the Giro was all the more remarkable because, on key stages of the race, his team was working against him in a bid to reclaim the jersey for Visentini.

Just a few weeks later cyclists prepare to line up at the start of the Tour de France – one of the toughest physical challenges in world sport. With over 2,000 miles (3218km) of racing in just 23 days (including two rest days), the Tour de France is the jewel in the crown of world cycling. As a result, it is the race that everyone wants to win. The competition is not only fierce, but relentless. What's more, the course is unforgiving, with multiple big mountain stages designed to separate the riders leading the general classification. The overall winner is therefore not only the rider who can beat the opposition, but can also withstand the many challenges the race throws at them.

Compared to the gruelling Grand Tours, the single-day, circa 160 mile (257km) World Road Race Championships may seem relatively straightforward. The reality is that the race is anything but. The final major race of the cycling season, the World Road Race Championships take place around the world on courses with dramatically different

Stephen Roche

Every year is different and challenging, but sometimes it comes together. I had a very bad 1986 due to injury and started training for the new season (1987) early. One thing that was very important for the Triple was that I was employed as a potential Tour winner and was being paid good money to perform in the major Tours. 1986 was a waste of time and the team pulled me aside and said 'you've only ridden so many days and we're going to have to cut your contract'. I said that there was no reason to cut my contract and that I didn't have to accept it. But to show I was serious I agreed that by Easter 1987, if I hadn't performed, then I would discuss a reduction in my salary. So I had a very important meeting in 1987 and had to have results for it.

But I didn't need pressure from the team because I was a winner – I still am today. The only thing I wanted to do was win. I didn't need any pressure from them to get me focused. I was very focused, I had just had bad luck.

There was a big presentation in 2014 at the Tour de France – they did a presentation about the history. They made up a screen of the 100 winners of the last 100 Tours. They said there were 57 different winners, so a number of heads disappeared. Then they said seven of the guys had won the Tour and Giro in the same year, and more heads dropped off. And then they said only two have won the Tour, Giro and Worlds in the same year – one of them was Eddy Merckx and the other was Stephen Roche. That's when you realise how big it is.

I think it can be done again. It isn't just the rider who is on form on the day who wins it. Other things have to be taken into consideration. For example, a Tour rider is generally a classy rider who can get over climbs and things. If, however, Contador or Froome wins the Giro and Tour but then the Worlds are flat, it's going to be complicated. But if they do the Giro and Tour and get an undulating Worlds, then they could. It would be very difficult for a sprinter or a flat stage rider to win the Triple. Years ago you had Tour riders, like Hinault, who were very good sprinters. But

above Stephen Roche seals the Triple Crown

everything has to go well for you. No injuries, the form, the team, the right tactics. There are lots of things that have to be taken into consideration that add up to the win. I definitely think it can be done, but not just because you're the strongest rider – everything else has to go in your favour.

The winners of these races have a little bit more of everything: more motivation, strength, hunger ... a little bit more. One of my big points was that I always said that there was no mountain too big to climb, and that second place was not an option. I would never look at a situation and say 'this is wrong'. I would look for the solution. It was always one of my good points as a racer. I'm very optimistic – sometimes too much.

Stephen Roche won the Triple Crown of Cycling in 1987. For more information, visit: www.stephenroche.com.

characteristics. As such, some years the course will favour sprinters, other years it will be suited to all-rounders. Instead of racing in their usual teams, riders race for their countries. Despite the rigours of a tough season, the event itself is incredibly competitive, with the 'big names' all gunning for the final major jersey of the season.

As road cycling has grown into a multi-billion dollar industry, riders have tended to become specialists in certain 'disciplines'. Whether that is sprinting, climbing or even single-day 'Classic' races, the emphasis is increasingly on producing results. The same is true for the 'big' team leaders. The pressure to produce results means that

many top riders will target one major race each year. An exceptional few will perhaps target two. Because of this some have questioned whether the Triple Crown of Cycling will ever be won again.

But it is only that exceptional few who are capable of claiming this Crown. Eddy Merckx and Stephen Roche have proved that. In all likelihood, at some point in the future a special rider will combine exceptional form with the healthy dose of luck needed to win all three titles in a single season. When they do, they will have completed a once-in-a-generation achievement. What's more, they will have cemented their name in cycling's illustrious history books.

Type Diving
Date Year-round
Distance up to 58.28m (191.207ft)
Main challenges Impact, conditions

Competitors say
It's like surviving suicide, and doing it with style and grace.
Blake Aldridge

Cliff Diving

There are few sports in the world that are as simple as cliff diving. All an athlete needs is a cliff, some water, and plenty of courage. But while the concept of cliff diving is relatively straightforward, the execution is anything but. Cliff diving is a test of nerve, strength, and the ability to read the conditions of the wind and the water.

right Cliff diving was popularised in the 1960s

In all likelihood, the origins of cliff diving date back to the dawn of mankind. However, it was first recorded in Lanai, Hawaii, back in the 1770s. Local warriors would jump off the cliffs into the sea to demonstrate their prowess and impress the local women. Kings even got involved, although for the most part they simply judged the winners of these acrobatic competitions. As time progressed, people around the world continued to jump off cliffs. Elvis Presley shone a spotlight on the sport with the film *Fun in Acapulco*, where local love rivals demonstrated their prowess by diving off the cliffs of La Quebrada.

While the plot may have been whimsical, the diving was anything but. In the years following its release, the La Quebrada Cliff Divers earned international acclaim – and worldwide television audiences – performing their death-defying leaps off the 35m (115ft) La Quebrada cliffs in Acapulco, Mexico. It is a tradition that continues to this day, with hundreds of spectators turning out every night to watch these divers perform sunset jumps into the constantly moving and relatively shallow (3m/12ft) sea water.

As diving garnered increased attention – helped in a large part by the inclusion of high diving in the Olympics – cliff diving underwent a resurgence. In 2009 the Red Bull Cliff Diving World Series was launched. Bringing together some of the world's best cliff and Olympic divers, the World Series now tours through a variety of countries each calendar year. Divers perform four jumps from between 26.5m and 28m (87-91ft), and are judged on the level of difficulty during the dive. Similar to the diving shown in La Quebrada, thousands

turn out to watch these athletes compete.

Whether diving from the cliffs of Acapulco or from a bridge in Bilbao, athletes will look to execute a variety of moves during their dive in an effort to impress. The three most common moves are: the pike (knees straight, body bent double at the hips); the tuck (rolled into a ball); and the straight (no bend in the body). These moves can also help competitors control a dive. If, for instance, they are travelling too slowly through the air they will often adopt a tight pike position, whereas if they are travelling too quickly, they will straighten their bodies to arrest the momentum.

All of these movements – and their corrections – are executed in less than three seconds. Cliff divers obviously gain speed once they leave the platform, and expect to enter the water at around 55mph (90kph). When they hit the water, the deceleration is violent and immediate. Within a second of impact their speed goes to zero – placing 2-3g of pressure on their bodies. Muscles that were extended are instantly contracted, while any body tissue that isn't hardened to the impact of a dive immediately feels the force of it.

This is where the skill of the diver comes to the fore. Of course, controlling their movement through the air is key to the success of any diver. However, preparing the body for entry into the water is essential for their physical well-being. Divers usually land feet first, although will occasionally enter the water head-first. Upon entry, abdominal muscles protect the back, while leg muscles secure the area around the groin. When a diver loses control it is not uncommon for them to

above The Red Bull Cliff Diving series takes place around the world

below Divers can
alter their routines in
mid-air depending on
their speed

suffer serious injury. It is said that a belly flop from
28m (91ft) is the equivalent of doing the same thing
onto concrete from 13m (42ft).

Of course, divers do everything they can to mitigate
against the dangers of the sport. Ocean swells and wind
patterns are carefully analysed to ensure the optimum
conditions for safe diving. Meanwhile, surface spray is
sometimes used to help both break the solidity of the
water and assist with judging distances.

Olivier Favre holds the record for the highest ever cliff
dive, at 53.9m (177ft). Rudolf Bok jumped from 58.28m (191ft)
but fractured his vertebrae on impact. Orlando Duque is
the undoubted poster boy of competition cliff diving. Duque
has not only won numerous world titles, but was also the
first gold medallist in Olympic high diving.

Cliff diving is a beautifully simple sport. It is also very
dangerous. Athletes train for years to execute complex dives,
and even then don't always get things right. When they do,
though, they wow the thousands of people who turn out to
watch them leap through the air with style and grace. Every
one of them is enthralled by the courage and skill required
to compete in one of the world's original extreme sports.

Orlando **Duque**

The basic training is diving – we are all divers. For high diving you have to modify a few things. We work different types of muscles because the water is impacted from much higher. There's a lot of mental preparation involved; I do visualisation, I do breathing exercises to calm myself down. On a regular cliff dive, naturally your brain tells you to be careful. So I try to calm myself and just visualise the dive so I am ready.

For the very difficult dives that we do in competition, if you make a mistake, it's tough to get a high score. But you can save it – let's say from a bad score or an injury. If I make a mistake at the beginning of the dive, even though it's only three seconds, I immediately know what is going on. You train yourself to react and adapt quickly so that you can fix the dive and avoid a bad landing.

Changing conditions affect you. We can take into account a lot of things – cold water, the sun, things like that. But when it is raining or windy you start thinking about that when you should be focused on the dive. You can't do much about it, but try to do a good dive.

I do get scared. It's not terror like a normal person who has never jumped will feel when they are standing next to me – they will probably be very scared. I am afraid, but I know I can control what I am doing. I have planned what I am going to do, and have trained myself to do it. So I can convince myself and think 'I can do this'. That gives me a bit of peace of mind to concentrate. Once I'm in that moment – focused on the dive – I forget that I'm scared and the next thing I know I'm in the air.

The perfect dive feels great. When you take off – and you know as soon as you take off – the whole dive in the air has a very nice flow. It follows every movement and each connects to the next – you know that everything is happening the right way. You finish all the twists and look at the water. You feel the wind and then all of a sudden you hear a loud bang when you impact the water and then everything is quiet. It feels really good. That feeling of fear that I had on the ledge three seconds ago is gone ... now I am in the water I feel completely happy. It's just such a rush. Sometimes you come out of the water and you're shaking. The contrast of those two feelings in such a short period of time is unlike anything else I've done.

Orlando Duque has won eleven diving world titles in his career, and was the first Red Bull Cliff Diving World Series champion.

OPEN TO EVERYONE

Type Triathlon
Date September
Distance 4,218 miles (6,788km)
Main challenges Injury, boredom

Competitors say
It's one of the toughest events that has ever been held.
Wayne Kurtz

Milan
Verona
Verona
Venice
SLOVE
Genoa
Bologna
ITALY
Florence

The Triple Deca Ironman

The Ironman is the pinnacle of many endurance athletes' careers, pushing them to their mental and physical limits. Some, though, choose to go further, entering races like the Double, Quad or even Deca Ironman. Then, in 2013, a group of the world's toughest ultra-triathletes met to race the Triple Deca Ironman – 30 back-to-back Ironman races in 30 days. The bar was well and truly raised.

right Athletes completed 154.5 laps of a (cold) 25m pool every day for 30 days

In 1974, US Navy Commander John Collins read an article that had absolutely nothing to do with triathlon, but would change the face of the sport forever. The article stated that Belgian cyclist Eddy Merckx had the highest VO$_2$ Max of any athlete tested. Collins took that to mean that cyclists were the fittest athletes on the planet, but some of his friends disagreed. After a dose of healthy debate the decision was made to settle the argument with a race. Collins worked out that they could combine the Waikiki Roughwater Swim (2.4 miles/3.8km), with a slightly tweaked version of the Around-Oahu Bike Race (112 miles/180km), and finish it off with the Honolulu Marathon (26.2 miles/42.2km). The Ironman was born.

From humble beginnings (15 athletes started that race), Ironman has grown into a billion-dollar industry with thousands of athletes competing in races around the world. And while the event may no longer hold the aura that it once did within the endurance community, it has helped to launch events that do. The Ultraman, the double Ironman and even the Quadruple Ironman have all become regular features on the triathlon calendar. But with every slightly longer race that launches, another even longer event is never too far behind. The Decaman (ten back-to-back Ironman races held over ten days) was the first ultra-distance triathlon of this ilk. Then, in 2013, the first ever Triple Deca Ironman was held.

The concept of the Triple Deca is relatively simple: turn up at the 25-metre swimming pool every morning for 30 days straight and begin an(other) Ironman. Those athletes that make it to the end of the 30 day race will have swum 72 miles (116km), cycled 3,360 miles (5,407km) and run 792 miles (1274.km) – a combined distance of 4,218 miles (6,788km).

Held near Lake Garda in Northern Italy, the inaugural Triple Deca Ironman brought 21 of the world's hardiest triathletes together for perhaps the toughest test in the sport. Every day competitors would complete 154.5 laps of a 25-metre pool, race multiple short loops on open roads to complete the bike leg, and then run a marathon on a course laid out in a local park (due to heavy rain in the latter stages of the event the grass became waterlogged and the athletes had to complete the race on a shorter, cemented circuit). By the end of the fifth day, 13 of the 21 starters had dropped out. Remarkably, after that day nobody else did – meaning the race boasted a relatively impressive 38% completion rate.

It goes without saying that all of the athletes who started the race were in supreme physical condition. But despite their exceptional fitness levels, the gruelling schedule of the race made recovery difficult and exacerbated the pressure placed on the body. Athletes had as little as seven hours to rest between Ironmans (if they finished on the limits of the 17 hour cut-off). As such, some were sleeping for just three hours per night during the month. Needless to say, every athlete raced in pain, and many had to find a way to race through injuries that were an inevitable part of the event.

The sheer physical challenge of a race like this is matched by the mental test it poses. Athletes were not only managing their performance while suffering, they were doing so on a monotonous course. Athletes swum in the same

below Managing the mind through multiple laps of the bike (and run) course was as important as managing the body

(cold) 25-metre swimming pool every morning, doing laps while staring at the same sponsorship signs. There were a few variations on the bike – on roads open to traffic – but the loops were very short and most involved a good climb. Finally, the marathon was completed in short loops through a local park, which were further curtailed to around 500 metres after inclement weather.

If simply completing the race is impressive, the performance of the winner borders on surreal. Jozsef Rokob was the first to cross the line of the Triple Deca Ironman, posting a time of 356 hours and 33 minutes. That amounts to a sub-12 hour Ironman every day – faster than the majority of Ironman triathletes complete the race in a single day. The fact that eight people were able to complete the event in total is a remarkable achievement.

The Triple Deca Ironman is, for now, the toughest triathlon on the planet. It is also one of the most extreme races imaginable. Running a single Ironman is hard enough, running 30 back to back borders on masochistic. To do so requires a unique physical and mental disposition – and the ability to tolerate almost anything.

ATHLETE PERSPECTIVE

Wayne Kurtz

I've done 90-something Ironmans and over the last eight years I've raced ultra-triathlons in Europe. I moved to the Deca – I did two in Mexico – and then we had one in Italy in 2012. That's what launched the Triple Deca. We were in Sicily and finished the race and the race director stood up to say cheers and said, 'What do you think is possible? Is it possible to do a triple deca?' It started as a joke, but six months later they sent out invitations.

The first week was hell. We went up a half-a-mile climb on the bike, turned around at an orange cone and did that 190 times. That was the bike course in the beginning because they were worried about traffic. So the field was decimated in the first week – we went from 21 starters down to eight after seven days. Mentally it was brutal. You were going up and down, and for 100 miles it was something like 9,000ft – it was crazy. And you couldn't gain time doing it – that's what broke people.

Everyone had a breaking point day. My bad day was day two. We did the swim in a 25-metre pool. I was about halfway through the swim and there was a beer sign at one of the turns and I thought 'My God, I'm going to have to look at this for another 29 days'. It hit me and I stopped at the end of the lap, grabbed some food and re-grouped. From that point I told myself to focus on what I was doing at that time; that was the way to get through it. Get through the swim, don't think about anything else and then get out on the bike. Even the guy who won nearly quit on day four.

Once you got through the first eight days everyone was in a rhythm. But you have to remember that this was a race. And the guys that were winning – it was incredible how fast they were going. From day nine or ten to day 22 – until the weather crashed – everyone got extremely fit. The times were dropping by hours per day. The top guys were going sub-10. You're getting beat up – the injuries were there – but you could get through it with less effort.

The last seven days we had driving rain and 50°F for 14 hours every day. And we were on this open road; it was wine season, with wine trucks, grape trucks and everything.

On the last day I broke down on the bike – I couldn't believe I got through it without dying! Not physically, but there was stress with all the things that go on. Everyone had an emotional moment that last day. I remember my last lap of the race well – I took it all in. We were running a quarter-mile loop because it was so muddy. The music was good, the crowd was amped and everyone was there. I crossed the line and the emotion of stopping was a relief, but it was also a little sad.

It's one of the toughest events that has ever been held. It was a race and people were going at it hard. Being able to deal with the mental stress of the injuries and getting up every day to do the same thing – it was like Groundhog Day.

Wayne Kurtz was one of eight finishers of the Triple Deca Ironman. His book, Stronger Than Iron, *is out now. For more information, visit: www.wayne-kurtz.com.*

Type Run
Date June
Distance 3,100 miles (4,989km)
Main obstacles Terrain, psychology

Competitors say
I've done a lot of hard things and this is the hardest thing I've ever done times 100.
William Sichel

Self-Transcendence 3100-Mile Race

Enjoy the slight downhill on Joe Austin Way before taking a left at the corner of the baseball field. Follow the pavement as it passes by the playground and the handball courts. Take another left at the corner of Grand Central Parkway and continue along the path as it runs behind the back of Thomas Edison High School. There's a slight change in elevation here. Take another left and run past the phone box along this stretch of road – just before it climbs a few metres up to the corner. One final left turn and you're back on Joe Austin Way. One lap down, 5,648 to go.

The longest certified footrace in the world, the Self-Transcendence 3100-Mile race is as simple as it is gruelling. Taking place over 52 days (from June through to August), a small group of runners tackle the 0.5488 mile (883m) course around a single block in Jamaica, New York. All runners are required to average 60 miles a day (96km), and the direction of travel – whether the runner turns left or right at the corner – varies from one day to the next. At the end of the race, runners arrive back at the very place that they began, so completing the self-transcendence 'journey'.

The brainchild of spiritual leader Sri Chinmoy, the Self-Transcendence 3100-Mile Race is not a conventional competition. Rather, it was developed as a way of enabling runners 'to challenge themselves and overcome their preconceived limitations'. Of course, there are winners and records. But the central premise of the race is based on a personal journey that pushes elite athletes through their physical and psychological boundaries.

Needless, to say, those boundaries are as numerous as they are formidable. First and foremost, athletes have to manage the sheer distances involved and the time it takes to complete them. From 6:30 a.m. (if they miss the start,

left Athletes complete 5,648 laps of a single New York city block

above A journey that ends where it began is one of life's great cosmic ironies, according to Sri Chimnoy

they are disqualified) runners have until midnight of each day to cover a minimum of 60 miles (96km) – or 111 laps. Throughout the duration of the 52-day challenge there are no 'days off'. As such, the cumulative fatigue is immense. Fatigue in a race like this manifests itself in a variety of ways, but perhaps most obviously it is through physical injury.

With concrete pavements lining the block, athletes are running on perhaps the hardest, most unforgiving surface of all. Impact injuries are commonplace, and even seasoned ultra runners will often experience issues during the event. Because of the time limits placed on competitors, most simply have to run through these injuries to realise their daily goals (the organisers do allow some flexibility in these time limits should runners really need it).

Perhaps more difficult than the physical barriers that the runners face are the psychological challenges to be overcome. The race is long (56 days) and for many it is hard to comprehend competing for such a long period of time. Once underway, simply maintaining the motivation to continue day after day on what is a very tough course becomes exceptionally challenging. Needless to say, this motivation becomes harder to muster as the fatigue kicks in.

To add to the physical and mental strain of the event, the course is 'open' to the public. As such, the pavements on which the race is run are shared with pedestrians, schoolchildren (there are two high schools along the route) and anyone else who happens to pass by. Runners have reported seeing people fall victim to knife-attacks, baseballs being thrown around them as they pass, and the constant need to check their direction as people unconsciously step into their paths. There is traffic too. The 12-lane Grand Central Parkway runs along one side of the block, with car fumes clogging the air 24 hours per day. It is a recipe for running frustration, and simply adds to the overall challenge of the event.

Of course, not every athlete who enters the race completes it. Indeed, many fall short of the 3100 mile goal, settling for shorter distances (which often total thousands of miles). But every year a number do complete the race. Some even do so on multiple occasions. Suprabha Beckjord

has successfully crossed the finish line an impressive 13 times and is also the oldest ever finisher at the age of 53. Meanwhile, Madhupran Wolfgang Schwerk holds the course record of 41 days 8 hours 16 minutes and 29 seconds – an average of 75.1 miles (120.8km) per day.

Records might be important, but organisers would argue that the journey that these runners have been on is even more so. A journey that took them along the same streets and around the same corners thousands of times. A journey that ended in the exact same spot as it began. And a journey that, for Sri Chimnoy at least, represents one of life's great cosmic ironies.

William Sichel

I've been doing ultra-distance running for 20 years and I've always focused on fixed distances – 100km races, 24 hour races, 48 hours ... that sort of thing. I always knew at the back of my mind that the longest one of those was the 3100, which is on a measured circuit. I wanted to do something that was an incredible challenge and completely off the wall so I thought 'why not do the 3100?'

The structure of the race is different to my normal races. I have raced up to 1,000 miles before. Normally these very long races are non-stop but this one had an enforced break from midnight to 6 a.m. So when I did the race I had to get used to this format. Mentally, I was almost treating it like a training camp – to get there at 6 a.m. and run as far as I could.

Normally these races are on closed courses, in parks on a 1km loop or on running tracks. However, the 3100 is what they call an urban multi-day race. It's open to the public and you have all of the normal comings and goings around you. At times the course can be busy with people, scooters and the rest of it. On a personal level I found the noise on the course intolerable, but I just had to put that stress into a box and forget about it. On one side of the course there was 12 lanes of traffic – it was the main road to New York from Long Island.

The first couple of weeks of the race went quite well and I got into the routine of running 60 or more miles per day. Then, on the fourteenth day, I got a calf problem. Apparently it wasn't a running injury – the support staff said I had depleted sodium and potassium.

I had a week where I didn't perform very well and was doing 45 miles or so per day – way under the required minimum to complete the race in time. By the time I got to the end of the third week I was 71 miles behind where I needed to be.

Once I got back running again I really got into the event. Physically I could feel myself adapting to it. I trained myself into running more than 60 miles per day; I think the highest I managed 67 or 68 miles. I did a negative split in the race (running the second half faster than the first) and that has never been done before.

The biggest challenge of the race was the psychological challenge, the sheer duration of it. You get to day 30 and you think 'oh my god'. I stopped looking at the scoreboard and the day number because I had to focus on each lap and taking it one day at a time.

I've done a lot of hard things and this is the hardest thing I've ever done times 100. The course is not ideal. It's an urban challenge; it's not flat – there are lots of ups and downs, the camber is the wrong way on certain parts. To put it in perspective, if I was looking for a course for a six day race and it was closed to the public I would eliminate this one immediately because the course is too hard. It's the most incredible physical challenge in every respect.

William Sichel is a world-record-holding ultra runner from Scotland. He completed the 3100 Mile Race in 2014. For more information, visit: www.williamsichel.co.uk.

SELF-TRANSCENDENCE 3100-MILE RACE
73

Type Foot, Bike or X-C Ski
Date February
Distance 430 miles (692km)
Main challenges Frostbite, dehydration, orientation

Competitors say
There are so many factors about it that make it so different. There's not just the perpetual cold, it's a true wilderness.
Karl Shields

CANADA

FINISH
Fairbanks
Central Circle
Twin Bears
Delta Junction
Eagle
Dawson City
Tok
Pelly Cross
Carmacks
Braeburn
UNITED STATES
ST
Whiteho

The Yukon Arctic Ultra (430-mile race)

Every year the town of Whitehorse, Canada, comes out to celebrate the start of one of the most prestigious sled dog races on earth: the Yukon Quest. A win at the internationally-renowned event is able to 'make' the career of any musher able to overcome the challenges of the course and the competition. The day after the dogs depart, and to decidedly less fanfare, a different race begins. It follows the same trail, but is run at a slightly slower pace.

The Yukon Arctic Ultra tracks the Yukon Quest Trail out of Whitehorse up towards Dawson City. Athletes can compete over three distances (100 miles, 300 miles and 430 miles) and in one of three disciplines: foot, mountain bike and cross-country ski. An entirely self-supported race (except for the single warm meal that is provided at each checkpoint), entrants are expected to carry with them everything that they need to survive in the wilderness. The list of mandatory items is extensive, with athletes in the foot and ski category pulling pulks (or sledges) in excess of 15kg (33lbs), as well as wearing backpacks that weigh around 5kg (11lbs).

From the moment the race begins, athletes follow the trail raced by mushers and their dogs in the preceding days. They do so between pre-defined checkpoints that vary in distance from 26 miles (42km) to 99 miles (159km) apart. In the early stages of the race, this trail is relatively well marked. However, as the athletes go deeper into the Yukon Territory, trail markings become increasingly infrequent. Indeed, at some stages along the route distances between trail markers may be as great as 5 miles (8km). Being able to navigate through the perpetual gloom (or dark) of the Arctic winter is therefore essential – and not simply to complete the race.

The Yukon in the winter can be a challenging and, at times, dangerous environment. With the race run in February, the heart of the Arctic winter, competitors can expect temperatures that range between -30°C (-22°F) and -60°C (-76°F). Add wind chill to those numbers and the difficulty of

maintaining athletic performance becomes obvious. Small mistakes are often severely punished, and can ultimately cost the athlete a finishing position.

The greatest threat to those taking part comes from frostbite. Exposing skin for just a few seconds in the extreme cold can be all it takes for an athlete to get 'nipped', particularly in their feet, hands or on their faces. Treatment is painful, and badly frostbitten athletes are forced to withdraw from the race every year. Frostbite is particularly prevalent in cross-country skiers because of the movement of the skis through the snow, which does little to boost the circulation in their feet.

This is not to say that 'warmer' weather is necessarily more welcome. In the Yukon, warmer temperatures tend to bring large quantities of snow. This can make the going extremely difficult. Dragging pulks – not to mention weary bodies – through soft, deep powder is an exhausting test of physical and mental resolve. Even cyclists struggle, sometimes averaging speeds of less than 1mph (1.6kph) through areas of deep snowfall. The snow also tends to make equipment and clothing wet, further increasing the risk of frostbite.

It goes without saying that the 430 mile (692km) edition of the race is by far the hardest to complete. Athletes racing this distance can expect to be out on the trail for upwards of ten days, with race organisers placing a 13 day (312 hour) cut-off on the competition. As such, despite the hardships of being out on the trail, athletes are always competing against

above There isn't much company out on the trail

both one another and the clock. All forego sleep during the race, competing for up to 20 hours per day.

Needless to say, the speed at which some athletes complete the Yukon Arctic Ultra is impressive. Casper Wakefield holds the record for completing the race on foot (186 hours 50 minutes) and Alan Sheldon holds the bike record (99 hours 30 minutes). Meanwhile, despite many athletes trying, Italian Enrico Ghidoni is the only athlete to have completed the 430-mile race on skis. He did so in 2013 in a time of 225 hours 10 minutes.

The 430-mile edition of the Yukon Arctic Ultra is as much a race as it is a test of survival. Of course, there is 24-hour race support for those out on the trail. But for the most part these athletes are alone in the Yukon wilderness. They are forced to push their bodies and minds through the deep snow, howling winds and perpetual darkness of the Yukon winter. And they do so against the clock, knowing that missing the cut-off times will lead to an enforced evacuation from the course. The Yukon Arctic Ultra is, in every respect, a true test of athletic performance – and survival.

below Athletes can expect up to 10 days out on the trail

Karl Shields

You have the temperature (-30°C or -40°C) and you have to take it so seriously. When you get out into the wilderness, it's extreme. You have nothing around you. You can't hear anything and it's a form of silence that I've never heard before or since. There is nothing: no animal noise, human noise, distant traffic.

It's a landscape that is beautiful and devoid of features at the same time. You have a combination of sky, snow and trees. That's about it. There's only so many of those combinations that you can put together before it all starts looking quite samey. So what if it is an incredibly beautiful landscape, Christmas-card beautiful – it's this perpetual version of it. You set off down a firebreak in the trees and it's an endless corridor. It's lined with snow, with the sky above it and you just walk. Then you run a bit. After you've done five or six miles of that, it starts to play with your head because it just doesn't change.

As the tiredness kicks in and you start to get sleep deprivation and the semi- or full-on hallucinations that come with it, the shapes that snow on trees can turn into are quite freaky. When you're on your own, surrounded by darkness, the head torch is on and lights up the snow and plays with the depth perception. I can remember picking out shapes in the snow that I could swear were goblins, and stuff looking at you. You have to keep stopping to check yourself. It's weird the way it plays with your head.

The longer the race, inevitably the physical maintenance you need to do becomes more and more important. You can't just get to the end of the day and expect to collapse into your tent and get up the next day refreshed from three hours of sleep in -40°C and set off full of the joys of spring. It doesn't work like that. You've got to look after your feet. You've got to look after your nutrition and hydration. And that is much harder when it's freezing – everything is.

And you've always got the feeling that the clock is ticking. It's a single stage race and it is different to multi-stage races. The length and timeframe is long, but whenever you stop you always have the timeframe in your head. You're constantly under a niggling pressure to keep on pushing.

I went through three cycles in the race. The first three days I was fine. Then a few things went wrong and the tiredness started to get on top of me and I struggled to get into the Carmacks checkpoint. I was mentally beaten up. I had to sort myself out to keep on going. Then I developed a bit of race fitness and I was getting more used to the basic methodologies for keeping going. They bought me another two or three days. The physical exhaustion started to pick up after six days – it got to the point where that was just grinding on me. I got into the Scroggie Creek checkpoint and only had 100 miles to go, but I was so beaten up and had had a frostbite scare with my feet that I was genuinely at the point of saying 'I'm done'. I just had to force myself out the door and tell myself that 100 miles is not a long way given what I had covered.

Karl Shields completed the Yukon Arctic Ultra on foot in 2013.

Type Bike
Date June
Distance 3,000 miles (4,800km)
Main challenges Terrain, weather, sleep deprivation

Competitors say
❝You just have to keep moving – you do everything you can to stay on that bike.❞
Mark Pattinson

CANADA
UNITED STATES
Washington D.C
San Diego
START
MEXICO

The Race Across America

The road is long. Very long, in fact. It climbs up over mountain passes and snakes its way through lonely deserts. It rolls through open prairie and negotiates the hustle and bustle of major cities. But there is no time to stop and admire the view – not for long anyway. Because this road is one long time trial track, and those competing on it are in a race against the clock – and one another.

above Support crews manage the riders body, mind and navigation during the course of the race

Bike Race at Santa Monica pier. Nine days, 20 hours and 2 minutes later (with an average speed of 12.57mph/ 20.9kph), Lon Halderman arrived in New York. The following year the Race Across America (RAAM) – perhaps the most extreme amateur bike race on earth – was born.

Since its inception, a few tweaks have been made to the format of the race (including the addition of two, four and eight-person teams), but the fundamentals of the challenge remain the same. Riders have just twelve days to cycle from Santa Monica, California, to the outskirts of New York – approximately 3,000 miles (4,800km). Along the way they have to pass through 53 checkpoints, where they

In 1887, George Nellis became the first person to complete a documented ride across the United States of America. It took him nearly 80 days to ride his 20.4kg (45 lb) bike from the East to West coast on an 'adventure to be had in no other way'. Plenty followed in Nellis's tracks, and the time taken to complete a crossing of the USA fell accordingly. Then, in 1982, John Marino decided to see if he and his friends could smash the record. Four men started The Great American

post their location and times. Other than that the race is a straightforward, single-stage time trial. Competitors can ride as fast as they like for as long as they are physically capable of doing so.

To put the distances involved in RAAM in context, the route is considerably further than any of the professional European Grand Tours – sometimes as much as 50% further – and riders have less than half the time to complete it in.

Like the Grand Tours, the climbing is ferocious. Competitors in the Race Across America can expect to tackle 170,000 vertical feet (51,800m) during the course of the twelve days. What's more, they do so on open roads, in some of the toughest conditions that the USA has to offer. The route crosses exposed mountain passes, wilderness deserts, rolling prairies and flood-prone planes. Changes in the terrain and the weather are constant, and riders have to adapt to them. To beat the race cut-off, they are required to cover 250-350 miles (400-560km) each day – way beyond the reach of most strong cyclists.

These distances mean that there is virtually no time to rest. Solo riders simply aiming to complete RAAM can afford to rest for no more than four hours per day (including sleep). Those looking to win the race often sleep for as little as 90 minutes during each 24 hour period. It goes without saying that this puts an enormous strain on the athlete. Almost all will suffer from hallucinations while riding, making it hard to control their bikes on busy traffic-filled roads.

This is where the support crew comes in. Teams chosen by the athlete are instrumental in managing them to the finish line. These teams control everything from overseeing nutrition and hydration (riders can expect to consume 8,000 calories per day, and drink 13 litres/3 gallons of fluid) to setting target times, navigating the route and enforcing rest when rest is necessary.

But while the support crews are invaluable, ultimately it is the rider who has to keep the pedals turning. They have to push their bodies on through the multiple layers of extreme physical pain and absolute exhaustion. One rider recounted

below Riders have just 12 days to complete the 3,000 mile route through RAAM's 53 checkpoints

having to cycle 1,000 miles (1,600km) with his head propped up by his hands after his neck muscles stopped working. That is the kind of commitment needed to complete the Race Across America.

Like any race, the competition at the Race Across America is fierce. Course changes over the years mean that comparisons of rider performances are somewhat redundant. However, in 2014, Christoph Strasser recorded the fastest time ever to complete the race in the Solo category (7 days 15 hours 56 minutes), at the same time breaking a long-standing record for the highest average speed (16.42mph/26.42kph). The team record was also broken in 2013, with a team of eight completing the course in 5 days 3 hours and 45 minutes (average speed: 24.2mph/38.9kph).

Many races claim to be the toughest in the world. For cycling, the Race Across America could well be it. A true race of extremes, it is a brutal and unforgiving test of strength, stamina and suffering that is far beyond the capabilities of all but a few masochistic endurance cyclists.

Mark Pattinson

RAAM is the ultimate ultra race out there. But it's so much more than any other ultra race. In most races you can get by without sleeping. But RAAM is a different scale; you need to be able to ride consistently and recover, and do that for multiple days.

You can't prepare for it; nobody has any idea how the body will react. You can't replicate riding 9, 10 or even 12 days with two or three hours sleep without just doing it in the race. So even with the best preparation in the world you still don't know how you're going to feel on day four.

The first thousand miles of the race are utterly brutal. You go through every single condition, every altitude. The heat, the cold, the desert, the mountains and the wind. If you get through that 1,000 miles, then you can re-group. That's typically the part of the race that blows people up because it's just so exhausting. And people think 'if I can't make it to 1,000 miles, 3,000 miles is comical'.

There are plenty of challenges through the race; the course is not made to be the quickest way across the country. It's designed to be a tough challenge. The last 500 miles is a stretch through West Virginia, which is 500 foot rollers for 180 miles. People often say 'I was looking at my time and thought I was going to ride under 10 or 11 days and was looking at my speed and feeling great', but then they lose 12 hours. It is really tough. For me, I'm in a racing position so I'm looking at the guys around me and thinking 'I'm trying to have the best race I can'.

Mentally, you just have to focus on the now and focus on the next six hours. You are constantly monitoring your body. I'm quite alert for the race and the competition and the weather.

But at the same time you're wondering 'why does my foot hurt? Why do my shoulders hurt?' After nine days on the bike, things hurt. Sometimes you make small adjustments and it goes away. All the time you just have to keep moving – you do everything you can to stay on that bike. Because it all adds up. You start taking a minute off to adjust your shoes and then you have stop signs and things and you lose six hours.

I usually feel pretty good at the end of the race – my body adapts as the race goes on. But I'm tired – tired beyond belief. That first night's sleep I'm out cold for 10 hours. And for a month after, your body tries to catch up. When you finish, mentally you just feel happy. You look back and it seems like a hell of a long time. And you're with a team, so up to 10 people have been through some crazy experiences. They've seen the highs and they've seen the lows; lower lows than you can imagine. So when you finish you feel like the sun is shining and everything is great. Physically everything hurts but that just washes away.

It's a unique event, it really is. You are being asked to do stuff which is beyond what most people believe the body can do. But it's within the reach of people who really want to do it – you just have to really want to do it. If you're not mentally determined that this is something you want to do, you shouldn't enter.

Mark Pattinson has finished RAAM four times, and come second on three separate occasions. For more information, visit: www.markpattinson.com.

Type Bike
Date June – September
Distance 2,745 mile (4,418km)
Main challenges Terrain, conditions

Competitors say
It's not going to do any good to stop, so you just keep pushing through.
Jay Petervary

The Tour Divide

For the world's strongest mountain bikers, the Tour Divide is an opportunity to pit themselves against the North American wilderness. Following a trail that crosses high mountain passes, snakes through sweeping valleys and negotiates harsh desert, riders test their limits against what many believe is the ultimate mountain bike race.

right Cyclists have to carry everything they need to complete the race

Running the length of North America, the Continental Divide is a range of mountains that separates river systems that flow into the Pacific from those that flow into the North Atlantic. In 1997, the Adventure Cycling Association built a cycle trail along the Divide, stretching from Banff, Canada, down to Antelope Wells in New Mexico, USA. They named it the Grand Divide Mountain Bike Route.

The Route was initially developed as a trail for 'bikepackers' wanting to explore this vast continent. However, in 1999, John Stamstad managed to complete the trail in 18 days and 5 hours. The standard had been set – and Stamstad's time would not be broken for five years. After aborting an initial attempt to improve on that record, Mike Curiak managed to knock two days off Stamstad's time during an event that he and six friends called the Great Divide Race. This race soon morphed into the Tour Divide, and the record continues to fall. Jay Petervary holds the current fastest time at 15 days 16 hours and 14 minutes.

Whether the rider is aiming for a finish near the front of the field, or simply hoping to complete the 2,745 mile (4,418 km) course, the challenges posed by the Tour Divide are intense. Many will aim to complete the route as part of the official race (starting at an event known as the Grand Depart), but organisers will recognise attempts completed outside of this timeframe. That is because this challenge (in the words of the organisers) is a 'web-administered, do-it-yourself challenge based on the purest of wagers: the gentlemen's bet or agreement. Nothing to win or lose but honour'.

above The trail
might be tough, but
it is also spectacular

This organisational framework sets the tone for the rest of the event: everything comes down to the rider. Once they have begun the race, they are expected to be entirely self-supported. There is no scope for assistance out on the course, and there are no checkpoints (nor are there prizes for the winners). As such, riders have to carry everything they need to sleep, eat and survive for upwards of two weeks out on the trail. There are towns and villages along the route, but many of these are small and up to 100 miles (160km) apart.

As the route snakes away from Banff and up into the Rocky Mountains, all riders have to be prepared to negotiate snowdrifts and sections of the trail that have been nigh on destroyed during winter storms. Of course, as they navigate their way south (there are few signposts, meaning that riders are responsible for their own navigation), the topography of the regions they pass through changes dramatically. Unless the area has been exposed to freak weather, the snowdrifts of the north are soon replaced by lush forests, which then turn into dry, dusty desert.

For the most part, the trail is covered in loose gravel or hard-packed dirt. However, there are exceptional stretches out there, and the race has a notorious number of clay sections. In the dry these areas are passable. In the wet, they turn into thick, sticky mud. At that point, riders have little choice but to carry their bikes towards the finish line.

But that finish line is a long way away. To complete the

Tour Divide in a 'reasonable' time, riders should expect to cover up to 150 miles (240km) per day (to beat the record they have to average 174 miles/280km per day). On challenging, variable terrain and along a course that boasts more than 200,000ft (60,960m) of elevation gain and loss, this can mean spending anything up to 20 hours per day in the saddle. Sleep comes at a premium for leaders of the race, and is usually done at makeshift camps on the side of the trail. In this respect the Tour Divide is as much physical as it is mental. Riders have to tackle extreme exhaustion and days spent cycling in solitude. For many, the lonliness,

coupled with the challenge of their surrounds proves too much, with as many as 60% of starters dropping out before the finish line.

An out-and-out sprint to the finish line, the Tour Divide is a challenge in the truest sense of the term. It is a race with no prizes. Instead, when the rider makes it to Antelope Wells they phone in their finish time and hobble to the nearest cafe for a bite to eat. It is an ending that epitomises the rest of the race: raw. For those that do complete this challenge, they can rest assured that they have overcome one of the toughest, longest mountain bike races in the world.

Jay Petervary

I don't think people grasp or understand what it takes to do something every day, all day, day in and day out. I mean that in the literal sense: all day. You spend anything from 18-30 hours at a time on your bike before you rest. In my case, rest means 2–4 hours tops before I do it again. We compound that not by days but by weeks; that's where the challenge is. The body can certainly handle it – that's up to the individual on how they prepare for it – but regardless of how prepared you are, you have to overcome difficulties. That is the nature of the beast. You are pushing yourself, you are on a loaded bike, and if you're racing or pushing records, then you have to push yourself through these difficult moments.

Any time I do the ride I present myself with multiple challenges and it doesn't come easy. You're never going to get a 'clean' run, meaning that the weather is never going to be great the whole time, it's not going to rain, it's never not going to be cold or hot the whole time – you're going to get everything. Every time on the trail you're going to have difficult things to deal with. Sometimes those difficulties last for minutes, sometimes for hours and sometimes they last for days.

Some particulars that come up are definitely physical. I've literally not been able to flex my ankles for several days. Dealing with that excruciating pain and trying to mentally block that out of your mind and having the confidence that it will come around and get better is key. You know, 'let me move my cleat around' or 'let me lower my saddle so I don't stretch my ankle'; these are all little things you have to try just to get through.

The clay that is out on course is also pretty famous. There are a lot of sections that are just straight out clay. And when that gets wet it turns pretty much impassable. You either have to walk around it, or if you do push through it, your bike won't be rideable; you're going to trash your drivetrain and rip your derailleur hanger.

I remember one particular night down in New Mexico and I was on a record run and I got shut down at 10 p.m at night, with a really bad rain and hailstorm that came in. It turned this great road into a really impassable one and it took me all night. I didn't sleep that night – I had to push my bike. It took me four or five hours to go 10 miles up this mud-encrusted road. It was pouring with rain and I basically had to hike with my bike, carrying it. There's mud all over your bike, it gets all over you ... it's just a real mess. You can't ever give up because there's nobody there to help you anyway. It's not going to do any good to stop, so you just keep pushing through.

I always say that you can only be prepared but you can't have a plan. A lot of people have a plan, but that gets ruined pretty quickly as soon as something goes wrong. So I try to be prepared as much as possible, I rely on my past experiences and I think that's what gets you through the Tour Divide. There's a lot that goes into it apart from the riding.

Jay Petervary is the course record holder for the Tour Divide (15 days 16 hours and 14 minutes). For more information, visit: www.jaypetervary.com.

Type Run
Date Year-round
Distance 4 x 155 mile/250km
(621 miles/1000km total)
Main challenges Fatigue, travel, environment

Competitors say
When I was racing I only saw the pink flags because I didn't want to lose the way. I spent most of the time on my own because I was at the front.
Anne-Marie Flammersfeld

Complete the 4 Deserts Grand Slam

Tackling one 155 mile (250km) desert race is the pinnacle of many ultra-endurance athletes' years – if not careers. There are, however, a select group of runners who choose to tackle four such races, spread around the globe, during the course of a single calendar year. In so doing, they join a unique group of individuals that have completed the 4 Deserts Grand Slam.

below Each desert brings competitors into contact with a variety of terrain

There are numerous physical and mental barriers to completing the 4 Deserts Grand Slam. First and foremost, runners have to overcome the logistical challenges involved. To become a Grand Slammer, runners have to complete four 155 mile (250km) races around the world in a single year. These are: the Sahara Race (North Africa); the Gobi March (China); the Atacama Crossing (Chile); and The Last Desert (Antarctica). Given the amount of travel involved in making it to the start line of just one of these races, competing in all four during a single year is an enormous undertaking.

Logistics aside, each of the 4 Desert races are enough to test even the hardiest ultra-runners. Every event is a self-supported, multi-stage race. Athletes are required to carry with them mandatory equipment – ranging from sleeping bags to food and hydration systems – as well as anything else that they need to complete the race. Water is supplied at various aid stations along the course, but that is it. As a result, most athletes will carry backpacks weighing in the region of 9kg (20lbs) without supplementary water. At the end of each stage, athletes camp for the night in the desert. While the surrounds are spectacular and there are physios and medics on hand to

soothe aching or injured body parts, the conditions are raw. As such, they are far from optimal for recovery.

Each of the deserts featured in the 4 Deserts Grand Slam presents their own unique challenges. Runners tackling the Sahara Race – the hottest desert on earth – are forced to compete in temperatures that can reach 50°C (122°F). Although the course is largely flat, the terrain ranges from soft sand through to loose scree and uneven rocks.

The Sahara is a world away from the conditions that runners experience in the Gobi March. In this race, the route crosses massive sand dunes, climbs precipitous hills and tracks through river gorges. Because of the topography of the Gobi, the weather can change dramatically during the race. Runners have experienced everything from extreme heat to cool weather and harsh sand storms. The significant

above Each of the 4 Deserts race attracts competitors from across the globe

right Trails are marked by pink flags

Anne-Marie Flammersfeld

In 2011, I was travelling in South America and met a runner who was going to do the race in Antarctica. At that point I had only run two marathons; I had never done an ultra marathon. When I went home I did some research and I thought 'Okay, there are four deserts. You can do it in one year'. That was my idea. No German had done the Grand Slam, so that was my goal. I started training in 2011, and then in March I started racing in the Atacama.

The hardest race for me was definitely the Sahara race because of the heat, and because everything was flat. I live in the high Alpine region of Switzerland and we never have warm temperatures. So I wasn't able to train for the heat. It was brutal, and my body started playing tricks on me; I had a skin problem and I was suffering a lot. In the Atacama and Gobi, there were a lot of hills and rocks to run up and down – conditions that I like. I am not a flat runner, but the Sahara is very flat.

You have to love what you do and love running long distances. You have to have the confidence that you can do it. And you have to train for it: getting used to running with a backpack; getting used to running or walking six days in a row without getting a lot of pain in your muscles or joints. And you have to take it one day at a time. You mustn't think on day one: 'I have to do five more days'. You have to think: 'This is day one, and when tomorrow comes I will see it tomorrow'. You can't waste time with your thoughts on the future.

When I was racing I only looked out for the pink flags, because I didn't want to lose the way. I spent most of the time on my own because I was at the front. From time to time I was able to recognise the landscape, but when I race I do it because I want to be in the first group. So I don't stop to take pictures. I had time to enjoy the landscape in the campsite between the stages.

I was hysterical when I crossed the finish line of the Last Desert. I was filming myself with my camera and when I look at it now I was saying 'I am running the last kilometre, I am winning!' After the third desert, the Sahara, I was really nervous to get to Antarctica. It was a long trip and I was nervous that I would survive and do well and stay healthy and not break my ankle or whatever – I wanted to finish the Grand Slam. When I eventually finished I was nervous, I was happy, I was sad ... a lot of emotions.

Anne-Marie Flammersfeld is a sports scientist and one of only two people to have won all four races while completing the 4 Deserts Grand Slam.

elevation change and difficult running conditions makes the Gobi March a famously unforgiving challenge.

So, too, is the Atacama Crossing. Athletes race through a lunar landscape that is as spectacular as it is bleak. The driest non-Polar desert on earth, the course reaches elevations of 3,000m (10,000ft) above sea level – meaning that altitude also plays a factor in performance. Like the Gobi March before it, the terrain in the Atacama varies dramatically and so the weather can be unpredictable.

To compete in The Last Desert, athletes have to have completed at least one of the other races. Unique, dangerous and challenging on every level, racing in Antarctica is unlike any of the other Deserts. The ice and inclement weather provide the obvious differences, but the format changes too. Because of the unpredictable nature of the climate, the Last Desert is not a point-to-point race. Instead, athletes run in either times or loops that vary in length. They can also be called off the course at any point. This simply complicates pacing and body management throughout the race, meaning that athletes have to be adaptable and versatile.

As with any extreme challenge, mental strength is the key to completing the 4 Deserts Grand Slam – regardless of whether the athlete is competing for the win or simply trying to avoid the stage cut-off times established by the organisers.

At the front of the field competition is fierce. Many serious ultra-runners compete in the 4 Deserts series, and some of the times recorded are exceptional. Because the courses change from year to year, it is somewhat redundant to compare these times, however, two names stand out in terms of Grand Slam performance: Vicente Juan Garcia Beneito and Anne-Marie Flammersfeld. In a remarkable year of racing, both athletes not only completed the 4 Deserts Grand Slam, but won every race that they entered.

Completing one of the 4 Deserts is a huge challenge, but completing all four in the space of a calendar year is a supreme physical, mental and logistical achievement. Tackling huge distances through different climates and terrains puts the body under enormous stress that would buckle many experienced runners. Those that are able to deal with the demands of the series join a unique – not to mention – small group of ultra-runners.

opposite The Last Desert is unique in both its setting and set up

Type Motor race
Date January
Distance circa 6,200 miles (10,000km)
Main obstacles Terrain, crashing, navigation

Competitors say
There is no competition mixed with adventure like the Dakar Rally.
Cyril Despres

The Dakar Rally

From precipitous sand dunes to perilous mountain roads, the Dakar Rally pits some of the world's best drivers against some of South America's toughest terrain. For all who enter, simply completing the race demands supreme levels of concentration and endurance. To win it, those qualities have to be coupled with an unflinching thirst for speed.

right A race and an adventure. The Dakar Rally challenges the world's best drivers across a variety of terrain

In 1977, Thierry Sabine got lost in the Libyan Desert while competing in the Abidjan-Nice Rally. While many would have panicked at their predicament, Sabine was inspired. After being rescued, he returned to Europe and started planning an extraordinary race. Just a few months later, 170 competitors revved their engines on the start line of the inaugural Paris-Dakar Rally. A legend was born.

In those early days, the Paris-Dakar was all about the personal challenge. However, as its reputation grew, some of the world's best drivers and motorcyclists were attracted to the Parisian start line. Very soon, it became a competitive event in its own right. Every year hundreds would start, and every year most would fail to finish. In 1986 – purportedly the hardest race ever run – just 100 of the 486 starters made it to Dakar, and there were seven fatalities (including that of Thierry Sabine, the founder, who died in a helicopter crash). The reputation of the race also earned it some unwanted attention. As the fragile political situation in Northern Africa deteriorated, competitors in the Paris-Dakar became the subject of kidnappings and terrorist threats. In 2008, organisers were no longer able to guarantee their safety, and the decision was made to cancel the race and relocate it the following year to South America.

And so, in 2009, the Dakar Rally was (re)born. The location was entirely different, and so were the challenges. But the fundamental premise of the Rally remained the same: to push the world's best and most tenacious drivers to the limits of their physical endurance.

Starting out in Argentina but always passing through neighbouring countries, the circa 6,200 miles (10,000km) predominantly off-road course of the Dakar Rally changes annually. A few things, though, remain the same each year. The Dakar Rally is a multi-stage race, and the competitor who registers the lowest cumulative time to complete all of the stages is declared the winner. There are four competitive categories: cars, trucks, motorbikes and quad bikes. Within each category there are a variety of subcategories, determined by engine size and modifications to the vehicle itself. While the cars and trucks are made up of teams of drivers and co-drivers, the bikes and quads are solo efforts.

The professional teams that enter the race each year have extensive support crews that help them to manage both the vehicle and their bodies through the race. However, the majority of the field is made up of amateur racers. And while all will call on the assistance of support crews in one way or another, for the most part they alone are responsible for seeing themselves through to the finish line of the gruelling stages. Some of these stages are short. However, the Dakar Rally is famous for its multiple marathon stages, which regularly run in excess of 600 miles (1,000km). During these stages, the bikes and quads are separated from the cars and trucks, allowing organisers to tailor stages to challenge competitors based on the capabilities of their machines.

While the length of these stages of course presents a challenge, it is the landscape across which the rally is run that provides the true test of driving skill and endurance. During the event, racers can expect to cross a range of different terrain: sandy desert with precipitous dunes; tight, and sometimes boggy, forest roads; wilderness routes lined with massive rocks; and vast plains of camel grass. Although the route is largely marked, there is always some navigation involved in the race. As such, there is little scope to lose focus – even for a fraction of a second.

Maintaining that focus is, perhaps, the greatest challenge of the race. Of course, an event of this distance is a gruelling physical test for those that enter it, however, the stages are such that the competitors have to remain constantly alert to the demands of the course. This need for mental acuity, on roads and routes lined with hazards, set against a ticking clock of a competitive event, is exhausting. Every year, competitors are forced to retire from the race because of mechanical damage due to a split-second lapse in concentration. Unfortunately, at the speeds the cars and bikes travel, racers are sometimes injured – and occasionally killed – in high-speed crashes.

Despite its relocation, the Dakar Rally remains a true test of driving ability and endurance. Competitors spend multiple hours negotiating landscapes that are at best challenging, and at worst dangerous. During longer stages the racers often forego sleep to improve their time, however in so doing merely exacerbate the challenges that lie ahead. Those that do make it to the finish line know that they have conquered perhaps the most challenging motor race in the world.

Cyril Despres

From my point of view, there is no competition mixed with adventure like the Dakar Rally. You can compete in the same category if you are an amateur or professional. In this way the Dakar is special. When you finish the day and you are in the camp and eating, you can't believe that everybody sitting there – maybe they race trucks, cars, bikes – has done the same route. This is special.

Physically, I think the car is less demanding than the bike. In the car you have four wheels and four shocks. On the bike you have two mechanical shocks and wheels. Then you use both arms and both legs – this demands a lot physically. I think the car is less demanding concerning the physical preparation, but it is more demanding concerning concentration. You don't have as much visibility as on the bike and you need to pay attention to all the rocks and trees, things like that. Attention is quite important.

For me, the hardest thing at the Dakar is to finish second. It might just be one more box up on the podium, but it is so many hours – 17 days in a row. In the past I have won this race five times and finished on the podium 17 times. And the difference between winning and finishing second is so small. To concentrate, to be ready every day, to figure out all of the problems during the race (like if you get lost, have a mechanical problem, a small crash, are tired), it's difficult. If you do it right and you find a way to solve the problems, then it all works and you are the top.

In Argentina, there are 500km of mountains in Cordoba. You have a lot of twisty pistes, which are really demanding for the traction and braking. Most of the time you have to ride standing up. I trained well for this and was waiting for a stage where I could make a difference physically. I would start the day and say: 'Today, I will have 600 or 800 corners, but I will try to clean every single one of them – braking as late as possible and accelerating as soon as possible.' In my last victory in 2013 I won the rally on this stage.

It's really easy to lose your attention or your confidence for 10 seconds. The problem is that if in this 10 seconds there is a sharp corner, it can be the end of the race. That is hard. One small mistake can cost you a lot. We do not know the track, we don't know the stage – we are forbidden to train on the stages.

It is definitely the hardest race. You can say that it is not the same now and that you don't start in Paris and arrive in Dakar. But what has been changed? Yes, we are in another continent. But my motorbike still has two wheels, my bike has one seat and one handlebar and there is still around 10,000km to do. It's a lot. Now the stages are more physically complicated – the navigation also. It's definitely the hardest race I have ever done.

Cyril Despres won the Paris-Dakar twice (2005, 2007) and the Dakar Rally three times (2010, 2012, 2013) on a KTM motorbike. For more information, visit: www.cyrildespres.com.

Type Run
Date A secret
Distance 100 miles (160km)
Main obstacles Orientation, hypothermia

Competitors say
❝There are so many reasons for you to stop and it's just so tempting.❞
John Fegyveresi

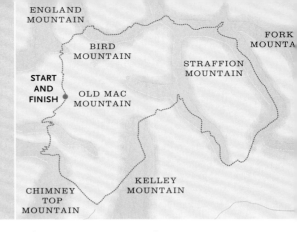

ENGLAND
MOUNTAIN

FORK
MOUNTA

BIRD
MOUNTAIN

STRAFFION
MOUNTAIN

START
AND
FINISH

OLD MAC
MOUNTAIN

KELLEY
MOUNTAIN

CHIMNEY
TOP
MOUNTAIN

The Barkley Marathons

The bugle could sound at any time during the night or day. When it does, competitors know that they have just one hour to be ready for the start of a race that will push every single one of them to breaking point. In a bad year (for the organisers), as many as three people will finish. In a good year, nobody will.

opposite Just 14 athletes have been able to finish the Barkley Marathons

Few races challenge an athlete like The Barkley Marathons. Even entering the race is hard. There is no website, and nor is there a correspondence address. Rather, prospective athletes need to know 'the right kind of people' to get the contact details of the race organiser. If they make it that far, they then have to submit an essay about why they should be allowed to take part. Only those who have convinced the organisers will find out if they are one of the 35 athletes who have been selected to race. Should they be successful, they will be told the date of the race and asked to pay the entry fee – $1.60.

The challenges have only just begun.

As athletes gather at Frozen Head State Park in Tennessee, the enormity of the race truly confronts them. Fewer than 2% of the entrants to The Barkley Marathons have managed to finish the 100 mile (160km) edition of the race. To do so requires completing five loops of a course that is between 20 miles (32km) and 26 miles (42km) in length – athletes and race organisers disagree on the final distance. Each of these loops contains somewhere in the region of 60,000ft (18,288m) of elevation gain, and the same again in descent.

To add to the challenge, the race is run over barely-defined trails. Competitors are given a map and some basic directions to follow as they run, scramble and sometimes bushwhack their way between checkpoints. If the trails are challenging, the hills are even more so. Some of the climbs exceed 2,000ft (600m) in little over one mile (1.6km) – a gradient approaching 40%. For good measure, the

organisers recently added a 400m (0.25 mile) pitch-black tunnel to the course. Every year, they like to tweak the event, always making it just that little bit harder.

To complete a lap of the course athletes have to pass between nine and eleven unmanned checkpoints (the amount varies from year to year). To ensure that there is no cheating, race organisers place a book at each of these checkpoints and competitors are required to tear a specific page out of it when they pass. Any athlete who returns to the start/finish line without the correct number of pages is immediately disqualified.

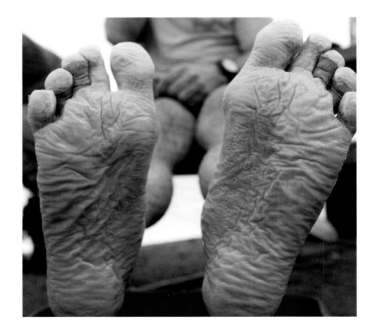

right The feet take a beating in the Barkley Marathons...

Every athlete is expected to be self-reliant from the beginning to the end of the Marathons. Apart from two water stations set up on the course, athletes are entirely responsible for their own well-being. Beyond the quite considerable task of managing their nutrition, hydration, clothing and general health through the race, this also involves orientation. Nearly every athlete will, at some point, get lost. What's more, there are no support crews (in the conventional sense of the term). If an athlete does lose themselves (which they often do), it is their responsibility alone to navigate their way back to Big Cove Campground. This is not always easy, and DNFs can easily spend up to seven hours just working their way back to camp – sometimes more.

Finding the track back to the campground is is not just important for those resigned to 'failure' (as the organisers like to call it), it is essential to meet the tight race cut-offs. Every athlete has to complete each loop within 12 hours, meaning race cut-off time of 60 hours. Although covering 26 miles in 12 hours may seem like a feasible undertaking, the difficulties of the course make it anything but. And while the terrain and the trails pose a significant barrier to completion in their own right, the weather merely adds to the challenge.

Occasionally the weather is friendly during The Barkley

Marathons, but more often than not competitors experience cold, wet relentless days of running. In some years runners have even experienced frostbite. As well as being uncomfortable, inclement weather makes steep ascents and descents hard, slippery and, at times, dangerous. Athletes have been known to break bones and tear muscles along the trail, and there is no support to help them back to Camp should that happen.

For those that 'fail', a bugle plays 'Taps' to mourn the end of their race. But every now and again – and certainly not every year – an athlete is able to make it to the finish line. In total (at the time of writing), there have been 14 finishers from 1,000 starters. Brett Maune holds the course record (52 hours, 3 minutes and 8 seconds). The year Maune set the record three people managed to make it across the finish line – the highest number in the history of the race.

There are very few races in the world that are deliberately set-up for failure. The Barkley Marathons is one of them. From the moment the bugle summons competitors to the start line at an undefined time in the morning, everything is stacked against them. Most athletes will complete a few loops of this legendary course. A very small number, though, will manage the five. If they do, they join an elite group of runners who have conquered one of the toughest running races in the world.

John Fegyveresi

It's such a weird mental race. In other races I have thought about quitting – the typical ultra runner experience when you're at mile 70 of 100. But Barkley is so different. It's like every component of the race is conspiring to turn that switch on. The year that I quit I came in more trained than the year that I finished. Physically I was more than capable of doing it, but there were so many little things that added up to the point where I turned it off. And it was so immediate. As soon as you decide that you don't want to do it anymore, all that you care about is getting back to camp.

I think that the way the course is designed is brilliant in that there are so many reasons for you to stop and it's just so tempting. The climbing, the overall terrain – it's brutal. It's not rocky or technical. It's just so steep and you're constantly digging in with your shoes and your feet are blistered and lacerated. It's very discouraging. Any one hill is a tough climb – even the 1,600ft hills. But when you put them all together, especially in the clockwise order, each gets progressively worse.

To finish, you can't think in loops; you just have to think '60 hours, finish the race'. You have to really want it and think of it as a single 60 hour loop race. A lot of people come to the race and say: 'If I can get in two loops, we'll see what happens' or 'If I can get in the fun run ...'. Once you make that decision you're already handicapping yourself. When I finished my fun run (my third loop), I came in and immediately went to my supplies. All these people said, 'Congrats on your fun run', and I didn't know what they were talking about. I hadn't registered I had finished three loops because I was so focused on getting five. You have to turn a mental switch on.

When I first finished, all I wanted to do was sit down. I wasn't sure who would be there – I had heard stories that when Andrew Thompson finished everyone had left. So I assumed that at 60 hours I was going to come in and there would be three people there. But there was a cool crowd there. I had become the underdog – the mid-pack runner doing the impossible. After I gathered myself it was unbelievable. I remember thinking – I have pulled this off somehow. All those hours of hill repeats and compass navigation in the dark.

In every aspect of ultra running, it's the hardest race I've ever done: the climbing, the mental aspect, trying to keep myself fit because there are no aid stations, managing my feet and managing my hydration, and the orientation. It's the hardest race I've ever done, hands down.

Ultra runner John Fegyveresi finished The Barkley Marathons in 2012.

Type Horse race
Date August
Distance 600 miles (1,000km)
Main obstacles Terrain, horse control, dehydration

Competitors say
" *The Tour de France crossed with snakes and ladders. It's extreme endurance crossed with loads of luck.* "
Lara Prior-Palmer

RUSSI

Orhon river

FINISH

Ulan Bator

Tuul

Boyd Kha

START

Hangayn mountains

Tamir river

MONGOLIA

The Mongol Derby

Around 1200AD Genghis Khan began a 25-year campaign that would see his army conquer a territory that was both larger and more populous than the entire Roman Empire. Khan's army was able to move decisively as it swept across Asia towards the borders of Europe. Their progress was facilitated by a network of Yams (postal routes) that enabled his messengers to travel at speed – much faster than his army. With a horse relay station (known as an Urtuu) every 100 miles (160km), messages could travel up to 4,000 miles (6,500km) in as little as two weeks. The system proved to be so effective that it continued in operation until 1949, when the Soviet government shut it down in a bid to erase the memory of Genghis Khan once and for all.

above Competitors are given small, powerful semi-wild ponies to ride

opposite The Mongolian countryside is as stunning as it is stark

Yams may have been consigned to Mongolian history, but every year a small part of the route is resurrected during the Mongol Derby. The world's longest horse race, this 660-mile (1,000km) epic dash through the wilderness celebrates the glory days of the postal system. The Derby features Urtuus every 25 miles (40km), where riders change horses and have the opportunity to refuel. The horses are checked by veterinarians at each Urtuu, and if a rider presents a horse whose heartbeat does not return to 64bpm within half-an-hour of arriving (an endurance heart rate standard set by the Fédération Equestre Internationale), they are given a two-hour time penalty.

This is just one of many measures put in place to guarantee horse welfare during this brutal race. At the start of the Mongol Derby competitors must weigh no more than 85kg (187lbs) when clothed. What's more, they are only allowed to carry 5kg (11lbs) of 'kit' with them – that includes everything they need for the duration of the event. These rules are designed to ensure the well-being of the 1,000 semi-wild local horses sourced for the event.

Unlike the large Western thoroughbreds that many of the competitors who take part in the Mongol Derby are used to riding, these horses are small, hardy and very powerful. They are also notoriously skittish, having enjoyed limited human contact during their lives.

As such, being able to control each of the 25 horses that a competitor will ride during the race is the first challenge. Most of the horses will bolt as soon as they are mounted, and once out on the course there is nothing to stop them from disappearing if they throw their rider. And being thrown is almost guaranteed. Broken bones are not uncommon during

above Once out on a stage competitors are on their own

opposite Rules around horse welfare are strict during the race

the race, and serious injuries (shattered pelvises, punctured lungs and broken necks) have been reported. In short, the Mongol Derby is no canter through the local park.

Rather, it pits competitors against one of the wildest – and most remote – countries on earth. To help them navigate between Urtuus, riders are given a simple map, a basic GPS unit and an emergency beacon in case things go really wrong. If they stray more than 12 miles (19km) outside of the 'corridor' between their checkpoints, they are penalised. Other than that, it is up to the individual to navigate a course that crosses everything from high terrain to wetlands, sand dunes and vast expanses of open steppe.

This terrain also attracts wildly different weather systems.

Competitors have to be prepared to race through extremes of heat and cold, as well as inclement weather and the occasional flash flooding that Mongolia experiences.

While the conditions in Mongolia are undoubtedly difficult, the physical challenge of completing the event is immense. Controlling one galloping semi-wild horse for a couple of hours is exhausting. Doing so four times during the course of a 14 hour day is extremely tough. Riders must cover a minimum of 75 miles (120km) – or three check points – each day to remain in the race. Riding like this places considerable strain on the body. That, coupled with the simple discomfort of being in the saddle for such long periods of time, poses massive challenges to any rider, regardless of their ability.

Because the course changes from year to year (largely to ensure competitors and their horses have access to water), it is impossible to compare winning performances in the Mongol Derby. However, the fastest time recorded so far was by Australian Sam Jones, who completed the 2014 race in 10 days. Winning, though, is just one of the goals of the race; the other is adventure.

The Mongol Derby pits some of the world's hardiest horse riders against some of Mongolia's remotest terrain. In so doing, competitors push themselves harder and further than any other riders on the planet in a true test of endurance and horsemanship.

ATHLETE **PERSPECTIVE**

Lara **Prior-Palmer**

The race is painful and horrible. People underestimate the athletic ability needed to ride a fresh horse all day long. You're riding from 7:30 a.m. to 8:30 p.m. and you're given three or four very fit horses that are galloping beneath you, meaning that you have to stand in your stirrups. It's very difficult to get fit for that kind of thing because there just aren't the horses like that in England. By the end of the first leg, I was in last place and thinking 'why did I sign up for this? It's the stupidest thing ever'. It's just so raw. You get broken down.

In the race you get left on your own with a GPS that tries to get you to go over mountains and through rivers. Getting lost was bad. I got caught in a flash flood on my own one night.

In terms of the most difficult thing, you want me to say being chucked off a pony. But that happens so quickly – and everyone falls. Quite often the ponies somersault in the marmot holes. I went somersaulting off one and thought it had broken its leg but I was lucky. I held on to it as I fell, which was also lucky. Otherwise they bolt and you have to run a marathon. But that was momentary compared to the ongoing pain of the race.

Each day a Mongolian herder humps you onto this pony that doesn't get ridden very often so it's jumping around. They try and hold onto it for you. And so you jump on and then you're on your own and you're thinking 'God, I've got four hours of riding and I could get so lost'. All the while, the pony is bolting underneath you. In England they bolt for maybe 100 metres. In Mongolia there are no fields or fences and they can just bolt for miles and miles and you have no chance of stopping them.

So you're on this incredibly fast machine – it feels like riding a lion sometimes – and you cannot believe how fit they are. Then they begin to slow and after two hours the pony has tired itself out so you have to encourage it while navigating. And there's just nothing around you. You pass yaks and sheep and you go mad and start talking to yourself. You have to learn to appreciate your own company. It's an amazing journey. You get to the next station and you wave goodbye to a pony that has served you well and that you'll never see again because it gets turned out into a wild herd.

Winning was unexpected – very unexpected. There were competitors there who thought I was a teenage ditz. In the end, it's very mental. People say they're setting out to win, but we're up against all of these different things and people forget about winning. I didn't.

Lara Prior-Palmer won the 2013 edition of the Mongolian Derby. For more information, visit: www.just-lara.com.

Type Run
Date September
Distance 205 miles (330km)
Main challenges Weather, elevation change

Competitors say
'You go straight into the high mountains and it smashes your body pretty badly.'
Nicki Rehn

Lyon
Aosta
Milan
Turin
ITALY
FRANCE
Genoa
Nice
Marseille
Flo

Tor des Géants

Every year the European Alps play host to many types of races. Athletes come from all over the world to challenge themselves against some of the most spectacular and accessible mountains on the planet. But amongst the melee of competitive events there is one race – a self-defined non-competitive challenge – that stands out from the crowd in terms of its raw toughness: the Tor des Géants.

Renowned in ultra running circles as being one of the toughest trail races on the planet, the Tor des Géants combines 205 miles (330km) of trail running with a staggering 24,000m (78,000ft) of elevation gain. Taking place around the Aosta Valley in the heart of the Italian Dolomites, the race crosses 25 separate mountain passes, each more than 2,000m (6,560ft) above sea level. Although well marked, this trail can be both uneven and exposed, with many sections skirting sheer cliff faces and steep scree slopes. As a result, athletes have to be willing to run technical trails in occasionally dangerous surroundings.

On the upper reaches of the mountains, conditions on the trail can vary dramatically. The race is staged in September, meaning that athletes have to deal with unpredictable late-summer weather. As such, runners must be prepared for anything from sub-zero temperatures, to snow storms, rain, wind and hot sunshine. A single-stage ultra race run in any one of these conditions can be challenging. However, managing performance on a multi-day race through a variety of them is exceptionally difficult.

The challenges are compounded by the semi-self-sufficient nature of the race. Along the route athletes pass by refreshment points serving food and drink. In addition, at certain places on the trail they are allowed to receive assistance from their team. However, away from these aid stations they are completely on their own. As such, they

have to ensure that they have everything that they need to
perform – and survive – in the mountains.

Needless to say, the list of safety equipment that
athletes are required to carry is extensive. When that
equipment is combined with the food and drink the runner
needs to compete in the event, athletes often end up
carrying relatively bulky rucksacks, simply adding to their
discomfort on the trail.

As well as managing their equipment, nutrition and
hydration, athletes face the difficult task of determining
how much time to spend resting during the race. At the
back end of the field athletes compete against checkpoint

cut-off times, with an overall race cut-off of 150 hours
(just over six days). Meanwhile, the competition among
the front runners is fierce. Leading athletes have been
known to sleep for as little as one or two hours during the
course of the entire event. Doing so is a brutal test of the
body and mind. Not only does this mean that they have to
maintain performance in the high mountains night after
night, but they also have to manage the hallucinations and
physical breakdown that are an inevitable consequence of
sleep deprivation.

While the weather, conditions and sleep deprivation
pose a formidable barrier to completion, it is the volume

of vertical ascent and descent that is perhaps the reason why fewer than 50% of those who enter the race complete it. Going up is tough, with athletes facing lung-busting ascents into the thin air of the high mountain passes. Coming back down again is, however, tougher. Not only do muscles suffer when descending steep, technical trails, but feet take a beating too. Bloodied toes, lost nails and large blisters are all common ailments shared by competitors, and in many cases these injuries are race-ending. In the instance that a runner decides to withdraw from the race they have to make their way to the nearest checkpoint (which could easily be many hours away) for assistance in leaving the course.

For the majority of athletes who compete in the Tor des Géants, simply crossing the finishing line is the goal.

However, at the front of the race, the competition for the win is fierce. Iker Karrera holds the current course record at 70 hours 4 minutes and 15 seconds set in 2013. In the women's race, Francesca Canepa crossed the line in 2012 in a time of 85 hours 33 minutes and 56 seconds.

This book is divided between those challenges that an individual completes quite simply because they want to, and those challenges that organisers pitch at some of the best athletes in the world. The Tor des Géants combines the two. Simply completing the course is to overcome a formidable physical challenge, racing it is to tackle one of the hardest trail runs in the world. It is a true test of running ability.

Nicki Rehn

ATHLETE PERSPECTIVE

I like to say that the Tor des Géants is a 330km race broken into seven stages. I don't think that the race begins until the fifth stage, so you have a 200km warm-up. It's taken me four years to realise that. I see it as a race where the first half you're trying to manage your body. It's very difficult at the beginning because it's such a hard way to start a race – you go straight into the high mountains and it smashes your body pretty bad for the first couple of days. You just have to try and manage it. By the third day, that's when you see who was able to look after themselves for the first few days. That's when people can run or not run, when they're broken or not broken.

I am a mountain girl and live in the Canadian Rockies so do a lot of mountaineering. From a technical perspective I find the mountains quite easy to go through – I shouldn't say run because there isn't a lot of running that happens. I can run down quite well, but a lot of people can't. It's quite technical and there are a lot of big drop-offs where you don't want to trip for sure – someone died last year. There are some precarious sections of via ferrata (handholds in the rock). The trails are in good condition, but it is very steep. You need poles to go up and in some places on this race I use the poles to slow myself down. I know people who don't come from mountain environments and they find it threatening.

It's all mental; knowing that over five days of racing your body will go through good times and bad times. It's about not panicking in those phases and saying to yourself 'I am in a really bad place right now, but I know I can fix it' and just being calm about dramas. For example, in the race in 2014, I spent 24 hours vomiting violently and not being able to keep any food down. But I didn't for one moment think 'this is a disaster'. I just managed it and dealt with it – there was so much of the race left to go. I had to do what I needed to do knowing that I would recover.

The sleep factor is one of the really big elements. Each person deals with it differently. Everyone has to experiment what works for them. Some people like to push through, get really tired and then crash for a few hours. I like to get a regular sleep each night – maybe 90 minutes at the same sort of time to build a cycle. When you're really tired and completely out of it, you lose it. You see someone who is sleep deprived on the trail and they're pretty much just crawling.

This year I finished at 5 a.m. and it was just me at the finish line. Previously I have finished in the afternoon and there were thousands of people there. It's mixed emotions at the finish – you're obviously proud of what you've accomplished. You need the idea that it's going to be amazing to finish to get you to that point, but when you reach it, you realise it was the five days of the race that were the best.

Nicki Rehn has completed the Tor des Géants five times.

Type Weightlifting	**Competitors say**	
Date Year-round	*"Your bones, your joints, your tendons*	
Weight up to 3,000kg (6,613lbs)	*... they're not meant to handle the*	
Main challenges Injury, weights	*load we put on them."*	
	Eric Spoto	

Lift Massive Weights

Weight training is one of the most popular sports in the world. People of all ages, shapes and sizes regularly head down to their local gym and pump a little bit of iron. But like every mass-participation sport there are an elite who take weightlifting to its extremes. In so doing, they are capable of moving some quite incredible weights.

above Strongmen have been lifting massive weights for hundreds of years

Since the advent of media and television, a small group of human beings have been intent on proving their strength by pulling, lifting or generally shifting the heaviest objects that they can lay their hands on. While Strongmen competitions made household names out of some of these athletes, individuals like Kevin Fast earned fearsome reputations by shattering various world records (Fast pulled a 188.83

tonne/416,299lbs aircraft 8.8m/28.8ft in 2009). Away from the spotlight of the media, records continue to be broken as both weightlifters and powerlifters tackle ever bigger and heavier challenges.

To trace the origins of 'traditional' weightlifting is to go back to the beginning of recorded history, with ancient civilisations in Egypt, China and Greece all referencing tests of human strength. In its current guise, though, the sport goes back to the 1800s when it was included in the original Olympic Games. Powerlifting and weightlifting became separate entities in the 1950s, and have continued to be so to this day. And while to outsiders it may seem that the sports are remarkably similar, to those that practise them they are entirely different.

Competition weightlifting involves two disciplines: the snatch – where the barbell is lifted from the ground to an overhead position in one movement (Vlad Alhazov holds the unlimited record with a lift of 566.9kg/1250lbs); and the clean and jerk – where the bar is lifted from the ground to the chest and then to the overhead position (Hessein Rezazadeh holds the record with a 263kg/579lbs lift).

Powerlifting, meanwhile, involves three disciplines: the squat – where a weight is removed from a rack while standing, the lifter then assumes a squatting position before returning to a standing position (Jonas Rantanen holds the world record at 575kg/1265lbs); the bench press – where the lifter lies on a bench, removes the weight from the rack and lowers it to his or her chest before returning it to the rack (Paul Meeker pressed 500kg/1102lbs in 2013 wearing a bench shirt); and the deadlift – where the lifter takes the weight from the ground, lifts it to waist height before returning it to the ground (Benedikt Magnusson holds the current world record – 460kg/1015lbs). Within each discipline there are various weight categories and equipment sub-divisions, and so records vary accordingly.

Of course, lifting those kind of weights places an enormous strain on the human body. As such, technique is as important a part of the lift as raw strength is. It is incredibly easy for a lifter to be injured – sometimes seriously so – if their technique breaks down.

As well as focusing on their technique, lifters work extensively on the speed at which key elements of a lift take place. To be successful, heavy lifts have to be executed quickly. This is to ensure a maximum return on the power output. As a result, as well as raw weight, all lifters will focus on speed training as part of their regimen.

Another essential aspect of the lift is breath management. Many heavy lifters choose to hold their breaths at particular stages of a lift in what is known as the Valsalva manoeuvre. This creates an air pocket between the abdomen and thoracic cavities, which not only helps to protect the core and lower back by increasing the rigidity of the torso, but also improves raw power output. However, this manoeuvre is not without its drawbacks. It places massive pressures through the body and many lifters burst blood vessels

below As well as raw strength, weightlifters rely on technique and speed

Eric Spoto

Powerlifting consists of the bench, squat and the deadlift. Your total score is the combination of the three, and the highest total in different weight classes determines who the best is – who the strongest of that weight class is. But then you have specialists who do one of the events. Usually the specialists have the highest number comparatively in the world. So I am a bench press specialist. We all lift, but as far as competing I only enter bench lift competitions.

The training is not only in the gym – there's a lot outside of it. The amount of calories that you have to take, the amount of rest that your body takes – you need good sleep every night. It's really hard on your body. Your bones, your joints, your tendons ... they're not meant to handle the load we put on them, the wear and tear. You always feel beaten up. Of course, you get the actual in-the-gym time, which is two to three hours for four or five days per week. But then outside the gym, in terms of prehab or rehab, believe it or not, there is more time outside of the gym than there is in it when it comes to the elite levels.

You've always got to be in an extremely strong state of body. When it comes to an elite lift, you've got to peak up at the right time. They've done a ton of studies on maintaining your absolute top-level strength, and usually it's about eight weeks. The goal is to peak for the exact week that is scheduled. You lay out a plan leading up to the meet, increase the intensity of training, but then you back off a couple of weeks before to let your body recover. At that point it's more about managing the mental side – are you confident and are you focused? On the day of the meet, you're loading up and being as full of water as you can be – you need to be super-hydrated. And then mentally you know you can hit it. The mental aspect plays a big part, but all of the mental preparation in the world isn't going to matter if you're not physically prepared.

It's weird, because you don't feel anything different with a record weight because it's been a progressive process. I remember wanting to bench 300lbs, I remember wanting to bench 400lbs. I can tell you about each day when I wanted to hit the lift – when I hit 500lbs the first time, when I hit 600lbs. It's not just like I woke up and thought 'hey ...' It's a slow process and it's not really shocking at all.

There are definitely limits to what people can achieve. Raw benching hasn't increased that much. In the 1970s Jim Williams was, they say in training, hitting 700lbs. He officially did a 675lbs. Almost 40 years later you're talking 50lbs difference. But I don't like to put limitations in my head to say 'I think I can hit this weight'. That puts a limit in your brain. Whatever that limit in your brain is, that's the most you can achieve. On paper, at this time, looking at a human bench, it seems about 750lbs – that seems about where it's going to stop, but you never know.

Eric Spoto holds the world record for the Raw Bench Press (no support). In 2013, he benched 327.5 kg (722lbs). For more information, visit: www.ericspoto.com.

around their eyes and in their legs as a result. What's more, if the breath is held at the wrong time, or in the chest as opposed to the stomach, this can also lead to temporary blackouts. Many practitioners of lifting have developed different breathing techniques to help combat the impact of the Valsalva manoeuvre, and equipment like weightlifting belts have been introduced to mitigate against it.

Since the dawn of civilisation, demonstrations of raw strength have captured the imagination of men and women around the globe. And with every weight that is lifted and every airplane that is towed, someone somewhere is training to lift just one kilogramme – even one ounce – more. In so doing, they are forcing their bodies to operate at the limits of human strength and endurance.

Type Foot, Bike or X-C Ski
Date March
Distance 1,000 miles (1,609km)
Main obstacles Frostbite, navigation, terrain, conditions

Competitors say
You have to just stoop down, put your head into it and keep going.
Tim Hewitt

FINISH
Nome
Arctic Circle
Northern Route
Faibanks
Kaltag
ALASKA
Ophir
McGarth
Southern Route
Iditarod
Wasilla
Knik
START
Anchorage

The Iditarod Trail Invitational

When one successful race begins, others usually follow. The Iditarod is a legendary sled dog race that runs through the heart of the Alaskan and Canadian wilderness. The exploits of the mushers and their dogs capture the imagination of a nation as these teams compete against the elements over a wild 1,000 mile (1,609km) course. Once the sled dogs have finished with the trail, it is the turn of the Iditarod Iron Dog – the world's longest snowmobile race. One week later, the athletes assemble. The Iditarod Trail Invitational attracts competitors from around the world to tackle 350 miles (563km) of wilderness trails. Only those that successfully complete the 'short' course are invited to return and compete in the big one: the race to Nome...

At roughly 1,000 miles/1,609km long (the route varies year on year) the Iditarod Trail Invitational is the longest winter ultra in the world. It is also, arguably, the rawest. A self-supported race in every sense of the term, athletes must carry with them everything that they need to survive the winter in Alaska. On the route to McGrath – the finish line for those in the 350-mile (563km) race – organisers arrange for drop bags to be left at certain pre-defined checkpoints. Fifty competitors are invited to go beyond McGrath each year, trekking, biking or swimming the remaining 650 miles (1,046km) to the Bering Sea outpost of Nome. Organisers do arrange a single air drop of supplies in this remote region of Alaska, but for the most part every aspect of completing the race is the responsibility of the competitors.

Not only does this include arranging nutrition and hydration 'pick-ups' along the way, but also determining their own route through the wilderness. Unlike many ultra-distance races, athletes are allowed to choose their own paths between checkpoints. Of course, all have the option

left Raced over 1,000 miles, the Iditarod Trail Invitational is the longest winter ultra in the world

of following the Iditarod Trail that is largely marked out for them. However, whether through their own knowledge or because of the advice of locals that they meet during the race, many will choose alternative routes.

For the most part, they do so without difficulties. However, in a race like the Iditarod Trail, minor problems can quickly escalate into major ones. Despite being permitted to use GPS navigation systems (although not those that allow communication with outside parties), following unmarked trails during the Alaskan winter can, quite simply, be dangerous. Some athletes have been known to lose their bearings in the remote terrain, while others have fallen through the ice while crossing rivers. Some have even been caught by open leads on the frozen Bering Sea. While nobody has died during the race (yet), such miscalculations can be severely punished.

That is because Alaska is a punishing environment in the winter. Temperatures along the trail have been known to drop as low as -40°C (-40°F). With added wind chill, it can easily feel like -60°C (-76°F). And the wind in Alaska not only blows cold, but it blows hard. Windspeeds of up to 100mph (160kph) have been recorded, bringing with them heavy snowfall and massive drifts that make the trail almost impassable. The area is also susceptible to a unique phenomenon known as the 'blowhole'. When the cold air of the interior meets with the warmer air of the Bering Sea, it produces a tornado-like pocket of hurricane-force wind, blinding snow and plunging temperatures.

The constant exposure to this bitter environment means that athletes in the race are particularly susceptible to frostbite. Because of the self-imposed limits on equipment that they can carry (if they take too much, it will inevitably slow them down), it is difficult for anyone competing to remain either dry or warm for the entirety of the event. As a result, most of the competitors heading to Nome experience some degree of frostnip, with many forced to retire each year because of it.

Fatigue, too, gets the better of many of those out on the trail. After all, as well as dealing with the conditions that the Trail presents, competitors also have to manage racing over 1,000 miles. Athletes at the back of the field battle to avoid the 30 days 23 hours 59 minutes 59 seconds cut-off in Nome. Needless to say, the competition at the head of the race is fierce. Leading competitors push themselves to the physical limits, sleeping for as little as one hour a day and only stopping to eat, or register their progress at check points.

Eight-time finisher Tim Hewitt holds the record for completing the course on foot (20 days 7 hours 17 minutes on the Southern route), while Jeff Oatley rode the Northern Route in a spectacular time of 10 days 2 hours 53 minutes. On the women's side, Loreen Hewitt holds the foot record (26 days 6 hours 59 minutes), while Ausilia Vistarini holds the bike record (17 days 6 hours 25 minutes). At the time of writing nobody has been able to complete the 1,000 mile race on skis.

The Iditarod Trail Invitational challenges some of the world's best – and toughest – ultra-endurance athletes against one of the most extreme race environments in the world. Most who enter cannot complete the challenge. The few that do have realised remarkable physical feat.

Tim Hewitt

ATHLETE PERSPECTIVE

The trail conditions can be very, very difficult or very, very easy. You're going to have trail challenges, mental challenges and even weather challenges – in any year in a race that distance you're going to have a mix of all of them.

The wind is the hardest thing. When you get to Alaska and it's -20°C, you can manage the temperature but you can't manage the wind. The Yukon River is two miles wide in places and you can't get off it – you're going into a brutal headwind. Or the blowholes along the coast on the way into Nome, where you get these hurricane-strength vertical winds. Those are the most difficult things to deal with and they are the only things that scare me. You can get into overflow or water, but that can all be managed pretty well. But when you get out there in the really cold winds and you're crossing 25 miles of sea ice with no shelter, that's challenging. You have to just stoop down, put your head into it and keep going until you get through.

I'll usually sleep for 3-4 hours and then get up and go again. Once a day I have to melt snow. When I stop to do that I have a freeze dried meal or get additional hydration. So normally I will stop to melt snow for an hour, stop to sleep for 3-4 hours, and then other than that I'm probably not going to stop.

When I start the race I know that day, two and three will be exhausting and things will start to hurt. My hips will hurt, my ankles and knees will hurt and maybe my shoulders. After day six or seven, your body gets used to it and those issues that come from soreness will resolve themselves. After that it's more a matter of trying to manage the body like a machine. You get the fuel in, you get the hydration in and you try to take care of the foot sores and the blisters or if a knee starts bothering you – you try to deal with those things. Generally speaking, with the exception of the year I went unsupported, I've done the final 350 miles substantially faster than the first 350 miles. I'm stronger, lighter and maybe I can smell the finish line a bit.

Every time I finish I say I'll never do it again but over the following months the memory softens the bad parts and highlights the good parts. But it's different every time. This year I did it with my wife. The year before that I went unsupported. Before that I was looking for the record. There are different challenges and I enjoy it – it's almost become a vacation for me.

Tim Hewitt has completed the 1,000 mile Iditarod Train Invitational eight times and holds one of the course records. He has written a book about his experiences: 8,000 Miles Across Alaska.

WET THINGS

Type Surfing
Date Year-round
Distance Varies
Main obstacles Rocks, Sharks, Drowning

Competitors say
❝If you're very gung-ho, you're not going to last five minutes. It's dangerous and you'll drown.❞
Andrew Cotton

Surf the World's Biggest Waves

Jaws, Mavericks, Teahupoo, Cyclops, Waimea ... even if you haven't heard of these legendary surf breaks, you will have seen photographs of them. They are the waves that capture the world's attention when they 'go off'. These breaks are big, they are dangerous and only the world's best surfers belong in the line-up.

below The origins of modern big wave surfing can be traced back to a single day in Hawaii

Nobody really knows when people started to surf. Peruvians claim that local fishermen started surfing waves to shore 4,000 years ago. However, conventional wisdom dictates that surfing began in Polynesia. Regardless of where the practice was pioneered, it was the Hawaiians who first adopted it as a sport some 1,000 years ago. And it is Hawaii that remains, to this day, the spiritual home of surfing.

If the origins of surfing are difficult to pinpoint, the origins of modern day big wave surfing are not. In fact, they can be traced back to one particular day on the North Shore of Hawaii. On November 7th 1957, Greg Noll and Mike Stange stood on Waimea beach and watched 12-15 ft (3.6-4.5m) swells roll in. They were part of a group of surfers who had come to the area to challenge themselves on some of the biggest waves ever ridden. After contemplating what lay before them Noll turned to Stange and said, 'F**k it, I'm paddling out.' The rest is history. Fred Van Dyke, Mickey Munoz and Pat Curren quickly joined them, and Noll is credited with having ridden the first wave at Waimea. Big wave surfing was born.

Word soon spread and Waimea became a mecca for surfers across America. Technological innovation opened the door to other breaks around the world, and in the years that followed surfers were tackling waves at now legendary breaks like Puerto Escondido, Killers and Pico Alto. With every break that was ridden, the search for bigger and more powerful waves intensified. It is a search that continues to this day, with surfers attempting waves that just ten years ago were considered impossible.

To survive in big waves takes years of training. Surfers spend hours in the water each day, becoming intimately familiar with their local breaks. In doing so they not only hone their understanding of the water, but they also learn how to take a 'beating'.

Taking a 'beating' means being able to survive when

the weight of a wave is forcing the surfer up to 50ft (15m) beneath water with only a snatched breath of air in their lungs. When this 'washing machine' releases them, they face a race against time to first determine which way is up, and then get to the surface for a breath of air before the next wave breaks. Waves travel in sets (popular wisdom dictates there are seven waves to a set, but science has disproved that). As such, if a surfer wipes out on the first or second wave of that set, they could be caught inside an area where another four or five massive waves are about to break.

Regardless of the training, nothing can prepare a surfer for what lies beneath. In almost every instance the waves break onto something. Whether that something is rock, reef or sand, it will be there. And when a big wave hits, it pushes the surfer down on to it.

Needless to say, everything is done to mitigate against risks and dangers.

These days a lot of big wave surfers will be towed to a wave on a jet ski (partly because some of these waves are travelling too fast to paddle into), and they will have additional support jet skis to assist them if they wipeout. Many also choose to wear helmets and inflatable life vests underneath their wetsuits.

Recently there has been a movement against developments like tow-in surfing, and many of the best big wave surfers are challenging themselves to paddle in to

below As technology has developed, surfers are tackling bigger and more dangerous waves

breaks like Jaws and Mavericks. That in itself is a phenomenal physical undertaking. These waves can travel at speeds of up to 40mph (65kph), and the surfer can drop as much as 20ft (6m) from the lip onto the surface of the wave. As such, to paddle in to these breaks takes phenomenal strength and exceptional skill.

There are only a handful of big wave surfing competitions around the world, but every time a surfer catches a truly massive wave it garners popular media attention. In 2012, British surfer Andrew Cotton surfed an 80ft (24m) monster at Nazare, Portugal – the biggest wave surfed (so far). The goal of many big wave surfers is to be the first to ride a 100ft (30m) wave. Aside from records, big wave surfing is defined by the people who have pushed the sport to its current extremes. Figures like Laird Hamilton, Garrett McNamara and Shane Dorian continue to challenge the boundaries of what many think is physically possible.

Big wave surfing captures the imaginations and attentions of people around the world. The photographs and videos of surfers willingly throwing themselves into the face of waves that could very easily kill them enthrals each and every one of us. What those videos do not show is the years of preparation and dedication that allow these men and women to challenge their limits in extreme, and often very dangerous, situations.

Andrew Cotton

ATHLETE PERSPECTIVE

With mountain climbing or running a marathon, it's a specific event so you can say: 'I'm going to run this or climb this on the first of March'. But who knows when the next big wave will be? It could be tomorrow or it could be in a year's time. So it's a very different sort of training. You've always got to be at a certain fitness level, but you don't want to be peaking or be driving to a session when you've done an horrific workout the night before.

Every surfer has their own spot – or the spot they know inside out. They know the direction the swell has to be, the wind, the time of tide. That is the same with big wave spots. I have mine in Europe. When a swell hits Europe, I'll be looking at my spots and working out which one of these places will be the biggest. Then I bat ideas back and forth with other guys who I know, and then I make a call where to go as late as possible because the weather changes so often. Then it's just logistics and having the right people to do it safely.

Every spot is different. There are some in Ireland and France that are much more easy-going; you know the way it is going to go. The waves are still huge and dangerous, but there is a 'safe' zone, a big channel and a specific spot where you take off. Places like Nazare is one of the more hectic places – there's no safe zone and the waves go everywhere. When I'm there my tension levels are higher, and the second you get in the water you're on the ball and you don't relax until you're on dry land.

On a day like that day, any wave caught was a giant. It was really choppy, imperfect, bumpy. All my focus was just trying to stay on the board and go down and I couldn't go fast enough. I went down and went down and then I just got mowed by the white water. And I remember coming up and thinking 'can you even get fast enough to ride these things?'

There wasn't an insane adrenaline rush [after that wave] – it was more like 'that was a big wave'. I got rescued pretty quickly and then it was still very much about wanting to get more waves. Sometimes I've caught big waves in other places and you get the adrenaline rush straight afterwards because you sit in the channel and say 'oh my god, that was insane' and talk about it. It wasn't like that. There were waves all over the place and we had to focus so there was no time to sink in. It wasn't until I was back on dry land and guys were saying 'that was massive'. Then you see the photos and the video and I thought: 'whoa, what are you doing?!'

I love it. It's you against the ocean. Not in a beating chest way. I respect the water and the ocean massively – you have to otherwise you wouldn't be a very good big wave surfer. That's an important thing to understand: the best big wave surfers respect the ocean the most because they get to surf a lot of big waves. If you're very gung-ho, you're not going to last five minutes – it's dangerous and you'll drown. The ocean doesn't respect anyone.

Andrew Cotton is a British surfer from Cornwall. In 2012, he surfed the biggest wave ever surfed in Nazare, Portugal. For more information, visit: www.andrewcotton.co.uk.

Type Kayak
Date May – September
Distance 3,351 miles (5,394km)
Main obstacles Conditions, weather, endurance

Competitors say
❝ *He asked where I was coming from and I said "I've just come over from Newfoundland" and he said, "Don't bloody lie to me, boy"* ❞
Peter Bray

Kayak Across the Atlantic

In recent years, the number of people rowing – or at least attempting to row – across the Atlantic Ocean has increased enormously. They are drawn to the Atlantic by the sheer scale of the challenge, wanting to pit themselves against one of the world's mightiest oceans, often as part of organised events. But while rowing the Atlantic is undeniably challenging, kayaking it is even more so.

right Only four people have been able to kayak across the Atlantic

Kayaking and rowing are completely different sports. On a basic level the direction of travel (forward for kayaking, backward for rowing) coupled with the use of one paddle (kayaks) and two oars (rowing) provide visible differences between the two disciplines. As a result of these fundamental variations, there is also a significant difference in the biomechanics of the sports. It is generally accepted that rowers are able to generate more power than kayakers because of the leverage created by having two oars that are both attached to the boat and moving through the water at the same time. Rowers also generate additional power by driving through with their legs during a stroke. In comparison, kayakers propel their boats with a single paddle that has just one blade in the water at any one time. What's more, the vast majority of that propulsion comes from the upper body (with legs primarily used for balance).

There is no race and no organisation overseeing attempts to kayak across the Atlantic Ocean. Rather, it is a true solo effort. Perhaps that is why only a handful of individuals have ever attempted the challenge, and fewer still (four in total) have managed to complete it. Kayaking the Atlantic is not only a supreme test of physical and mental strength, but it demands a healthy dose of luck, too.

While most organised Atlantic Ocean rows begin in the Canary Islands and end in Antigua, kayakers can start and finish wherever they choose. As such, the two most recent successful attempts have begun and ended in completely different parts of the world. In 2001, Peter Bray completed a 3,000-mile (4,800km) 76-day journey from Newfoundland to Ireland. In 2011, Aleksander Doba completed a crossing from Senegal to Brazil (3,351 miles/5,394km) in 99 days. Two men preceded Bray and Doba, Franz Romer in 1928 and Hannes Lindemann in 1956 (the latter with the occasional aid of a sail).

Spending upwards of two months kayaking across the ocean is a massive logistical operation. Because attempts have hitherto been solo and unsupported, kayakers have been forced to carry with them all of the food, water and equipment needed for survival throughout their journey. As such, they need to plan for a certain number of days at sea, and ensure that they hit their targets to avoid running dangerously low on essential supplies.

But the Atlantic Ocean is a fickle foe. As with any enormous body of water, there are days when it is calm and peaceful, and days where it is prone to thick fog and massive storms. While the former are welcomed, the latter pose serious problems for kayakers, and at the very least can drive them off-course. Ocean storms bring with them heavy seas that can not only capsize the boat, but damage it too. If the kayaker is unable to repair that damage, they can spend days waiting to be rescued. During his first attempt at crossing the Atlantic, Bray was forced to spend 32 hours in freezing water after his kayak was irreparably damaged.

As well as storms, kayakers often have to deal with the

Peter Bray

I'd paddled around Great Britain with a partially sighted guy, and when we were around the west coast of Scotland we had to paddle across one of the fjords and we were nearly run over by a super tanker. I said, 'It's got to be easier than this in the Atlantic!' That sowed the seed. When I got back I had a look at it, and, yes, it had been crossed in the South, but nobody had done the North and so I thought 'I'll do the North – from Newfoundland to Southern Ireland'.

The crossing is horrendous. I had fog almost all of the way across. Anything that could break did break. The GPS blew up after two days in a cloud of smoke, so it was all on a compass: if it pointed east, I went east. The fog plays tricks on your mind. You actually believe that you're on a 45 degree angle and that you're going around in circles and things. You've got to keep saying to yourself 'the compass is right, the compass is right' and just keep watching it.

I lost three stone in weight. Physically I knew what I was going into so I put weight on. Leicester University said I needed to eat 6,000 calories per day, which I couldn't do. I just couldn't eat that much food. So I lost the weight. But I was never hungry.

Out of the mental and physical challenges, the mental was tougher than the physical. Physically I achieved what I wanted to. I knew I would be sitting in the same position and didn't want sores so I used a beanbag – that proved to be well worth it. I got a few salt sores from the rubbing of my clothing, but physically the body was great. Mentally it was a challenge. The focus was on proving to everyone that it could be done, having been ripped apart the year before.

It was really strange when I finished. I was so chuffed. The first guy I met was a professor. He asked where I went and I said 'I've just come over from Newfoundland' and he said, 'Don't bloody lie to me, boy'. As I climbed up the ladder, he said, 'I'll give you a hand', and I said, 'You cannot touch me until I make a step'. Because I remember when one man rowed to Australia and they helped him at the end people said he had had assistance. So I took a step and fell flat on my face! I had no legs – they had gone.

Peter Bray paddled across the Atlantic Ocean in 2001. For a long time his was the longest open water paddle in history. For more information, visit: www.peterbrayadventurer.com.

WET THINGS
116

challenges presented by their fellow ocean travellers. Wildlife does sometimes provide welcome companionship, but whales have occasionally capsized small boats and sharks do attack them. Meanwhile, super tankers – which are common in the Atlantic – rarely stop for passing traffic and produce waves big enough to flip or submerge an ocean kayak.

But for all the extrinsic variables that can impact a crossing, it is the simple physical challenge of kayaking the Atlantic that trumps everything else. Kayaking is a notoriously challenging sport in its own right. To kayak for anything up to 20 hours per day, every day, for more than two months with limited food and water is an extreme test of human endurance. To add to the physical discomfort of the crossing, salt sores are a painful – albeit common – companion, exacerbated by multiple months in a sedentary position.

Kayaking across the Atlantic Ocean is tough. It not only requires extreme levels of physical fitness, but a mental fortitude that is beyond the capabilities of most people. What's more, it demands a healthy dose of luck. Because while weather checks and analysis of patterns can indicate the optimum time to tackle this mighty ocean, there are no guarantees. What's more, even when the weather is kind, it is very rare for a crossing to be completed without encountering the occasional storm, disruptive currents or freak waves. That, perhaps, is part of the attraction for those seeking an extreme challenge: the knowledge that the odds are loaded against them, a lone figure on an unpredictable ocean.

below Peter Bray successfully crossed the North Atlantic at his second attempt

Type Swim
Date February – April
Distance 3,274 miles (5,268km)
Main obstacles Conditions, wildlife, illness

Competitors say
❝The Amazon is the Amazon; it is the most dangerous river in the world.❞
Martin Strel

Swim the Length of the Amazon

Swimming the length of the Amazon is to tackle the world's mightiest river head on. It is a swim fraught with difficulties and dangers, and one that brings the athlete face to face with some of the world's most dangerous animals. A swim of this magnitude is not only a formidable physical challenge, it is a test of courage, skill and strength unlike any other open water swim in the world.

below Martin Strel swam the length of the Amazon in 66 days

Because of its glacial beginnings high in the Peruvian Mountains, it is impossible to swim the Amazon River from source to sea. Instead, attempts have (so far) begun at Atalaya, Peru. From this starting point, the swimmer follows the current of the main river until they reach the city of Belem, Brazil, close to the mouth of the Amazon where some 209,000 cubic metres per second of water are deposited into the Atlantic Ocean. By the time the swimmer reaches Belem, they will have covered 3,274 miles (5,268km).

Famous big river swimmer Martin Strel pioneered this route during a well-documented 66-day expedition in 2007. Serbian Darko Novovic claims to have bettered Strel's time – although there have been a number of questions raised about his attempt – completing the same swim in just 46 days in 2010.

There are numerous reasons why there has only been one successful (verified) attempt to swim the Amazon. First and foremost, there is the distance the swimmer has to cover. Despite being assisted by the swift-flowing current (it would be physically impossible to swim the length of the river against it), it is a formidable undertaking. In the upper stretches of the river, where the current is faster but rapids and whirlpools are common, Strel was able to average around 55 miles (90km) per day. As the river widened in the Amazon basin, the current slowed and the distance he covered each day reduced accordingly. Regardless of the speed of the river, Strel spent up to 12 hours per day in the water (with his team estimating he completed 30,000 swim strokes each day). Over a 66-day period, that is a huge physical undertaking. Pain during the swim was a constant, and the mental management of it was essential.

The physical pain of swimming for that length of time is exacerbated by the conditions both in and along the river. The Amazon skirts the equator during the early stages of the swim, and the heat is intense. Sunburn is a constant and uncomfortable reality for both the swimmer and the team (Strel's support crew improvised a face mask for him to help mitigate against it).

As well as the heat, the river carries large quantities of soil and sediment, which invariably works its way into the wetsuit. This builds around the areas where most movement occurs, causing sores and open wounds.

To compound the physical discomfort of an Amazon river swim, it is a mentally unnerving undertaking. Nearly all of the challenges in this book carry with them an element of danger. Few, however, bring the athlete into as close proximity with uncontrollable variables as an attempt at the Amazon. For starters, the river is a dangerous body of water. Whirlpools and rapids are common in its upper reaches, while on its lower stretches it is prone to large waves and tidal bores carrying flotsam and jetsam.

Below the surface of the water there are plenty of animals that pose a very real threat to the health and safety of the swimmer. Bull sharks, stingray, anaconda and crocodiles are some of the famous predators that line the banks and lurk in the depths of the river. Piranhas, too, live up to their fearsome reputation, gleefully attacking any passing swimmers. During his swim, Strel was bitten by them on numerous occasions, and his team were forced to develop ways of distracting them as he swam by (including dumping blood into the water).

But it is the smaller critters that frequent the Amazon basin which are more likely to cause a swimmer real problems. Malaria and dengue fever are commonplace throughout the river, while bites from animals like botfly regularly cause severe discomfort. Then there is the parasitic candiru fish. During his journey, Strel repeatedly discussed his fears of this freshwater catfish. Legend has it that it will swim into a man's urethra and can only be removed surgically. Whether these fears are real or imagined, they place an added burden on a weary mind.

Swimming the length of the Amazon is a formidable challenge that is beyond the capacity of most people. It requires enormous reserves of physical strength. It necessitates the ability to control the mind through periods of fatigue, discomfort and pain. And it requires a singular vision to complete the kind of challenge that rightly garners plaudits and honours around the world. The Amazon is the mightiest of the world's rivers, and only the bravest – and mightiest – swimmers are qualified to attempt this swim.

left Strel's team had to improvise a face mask to protect him from sunburn

below What lies beneath... the local wildlife plays a role in any Amazon swim

right River traffic and massive waves added additional challenges in the latter stages of the swim

Martin Strel

In my head, it was impossible to swim the Amazon. After the Danube and Mississippi swims, I said to myself, 'The Amazon is simply too dangerous'. This river is something special. It is for animals and indigenous tribes and there are too many tropical diseases.

Then, when I finished the Yangtze Swim, I said to myself, 'Okay, Martin, let's go to see the Amazon'. That was the first step. I was told by everyone to go home because nobody swims the river and they said I would die. And in my heart it seemed impossible. Then the second time I was there I said to myself, 'Okay, let's do it'.

It was hard to say yes at the beginning but now, seven years later, I can say that I was right.

When you jump in the river everything is against you. This is not like the Danube or Mississippi. The Amazon is the Amazon; it is the most dangerous river in the world. You have so many tropical diseases. You have indigenous tribes, some are friendly and some are unfriendly. You have the bull shark, a crazy, dangerous shark. Many snakes. Candiru. Piranhas. Spiders. Even the people in your team – because they are together for so many days in the boat – find it difficult with the high humidity, the rain and the lack of comfort.

And you have to survive swimming twelve hours every day. At the beginning it was a bit easier. The first day I swam 102km, which was a surprise for me and my team. There was a huge storm and we were very lucky. We had maps but the maps were wrong because the river changed every day.

Every morning it was hard for me. I was in pain and the first hour was terrible before sunrise. After breakfast I would say to myself, 'Martin, it is another day, you have to swim 12 hours. You decided to swim the Amazon so don't say I am tired or I am sick or I have problems, just swim. You have to swim six hours to lunch and then 20 minutes break and then swim six hours again. Don't say anything, just swim. It was your decision, just swim.' That was in my head every day. There was no excuse. I had to be in the water and swim. It was no use saying 'I am tired' or 'I am sick' or 'I have problems'. All of the people in the boat had problems. Some were in hospital, some homesick. This is the jungle.

After 66 days, the last day in Belem was Easter Day – I didn't know that – and 500,000 people were waiting for me and, wow, that was emotional. But for me it was just the last day. It was very wavy and I nearly drowned. Luckily, that didn't happen.

Martin Strel was the first person to swim the length of the Amazon River. For more information on the swim, visit amazonswim.com, and for more on Martin Strel, visit: www.strelswimming.com.

Type Breath-hold
Date Year round
Time 23 minutes 01 second
Main obstacles CO$_2$, death

Competitors say

There is no pain – just your perception of pain ... sometimes I leave my body and view it from three feet above.
Goran Čolak

Static Apnoea

Almost every human being has, at one point or another, practised static apnoea. It is quite simply the process of holding your breath while remaining completely still. But while many people struggle to hold their breath beyond 90 seconds (even physically fit athletes can struggle to go much beyond two minutes), there is a group of freedivers who far exceed these times. In fact, in recent years – with the addition of pure oxygen at static apnoea record attempts – the current world record stands at a staggering 23 minutes and 01 second.

below Controlling the mind is the key to a successful attempt

Although static apnoea can be practised both on land and in the water, every record attempt has been made while the athlete is submerged. There is a simple reason for this: upon entering water the human body undergoes a change that allows it to retain oxygen for longer. The mammalian dive reflex, which is common to every mammal on earth, triggers a number of reactions within the body: most importantly, vasoconstriction, which causes the blood vessels to narrow, helping to conserve blood in the vital organs (lungs, heart and brain); while a reduction in the heart rate allows the body to conserve oxygen levels, enabling a person to survive for longer without breathing.

While the mammalian dive reflex enables every human being (regardless of their fitness) to function effectively underwater, it goes without saying that those aiming for records in the discipline train their bodies to perform under duress. Physical training allows them to expand their lung capacity, and to habituate their bodies to the high levels of CO$_2$ that will develop during a long static apnoea attempt.

Mental training is as important as physical. All freedivers stress the importance of controlling the mind to the point where it is clear of thoughts during a dive. Of course this allows them to focus on their performance. But it also allows them to prolong it; brainwaves use up oxygen and therefore shorten the amount of time a freediver can stay under. To achieve this state of 'calm', athletes practise yoga, meditation and breath management (or a mix of the three). The latter is particularly important in the final stages of the build-up to the attempt.

In preparation for a static apnoea attempt divers will breathe deeply, making full use of the diaphragm. For an oxygenated static apnoea attempt they saturate the blood with oxygen by breathing pure gas beforehand. Once the

below There are
massive differences
in the world record
on land and in
the water

lungs are full, they then engage in 'lung packing', a technique whereby the diver closes their throat but continues to take in air cheekfuls at a time and force it down into the lungs. Some studies have suggested that lung packing enables a diver to add up to three litres of volume to their lung capacity.

When they have maximised the amount of oxygen in their system, the clock begins.

From the outside, a static apnoea attempt looks relatively straightforward. The diver is usually submerged in a shallow pool with light weights around his or her ankles to counteract the buoyancy of the lungs (although some choose to float on the surface of the water). Meanwhile, a support diver monitors their well-being while giving them regular updates on their progress.

As the clock ticks along, a static apnoea attempt eventually becomes a battle between body and mind. To reach their goal the diver has to remain calm and focused. However, despite the lung-packing, around halfway through the dive the body starts to crave oxygen as it becomes saturated with CO_2. When this happens, involuntary diaphragm contractions – the body's attempt to force oxygen into the system – begin. Uncomfortable and inevitable, static apnoea practitioners have to manage their mind throughout these contractions. The longer the body goes without oxygen, the greater the

frequency of them. Towards the end of an attempt they are near-permanent. At the same time, it is not uncommon for the brain to start struggling because of an oxygen deficiency. In extreme circumstances a diver can become confused, experience tunnel vision and in some cases black out.

There are two schools of static apnoea practitioners. 'Pure' static apnoea involves simply breathing 'normal' air (which is 20.8% oxygen) before a breath hold. Serbian Branko Petrović holds the world record at 11 minutes 54 seconds. In recent years, divers have been allowed to make use of pure oxygen for 30 minutes before a dive, and so flush the nitrogen and carbon dioxide out of their system. Goran Čolak holds the current world record in this discipline: 23 minutes 01 second.

It goes without saying that there are very real risks associated with holding your breath for such an extended period of time. What's more, as the 'extreme' end of the field develops, little is known about the long-term impacts of prolonged static apnoea attempts upon the human body. However, to be able to hold your breath in excess of 10 minutes on normal air and 23 minutes on pure oxygen is an incredible physical achievement. It demands complete control of the mind, and the ability to push the body far beyond conventional norms.

Goran Čolak

ATHLETE PERSPECTIVE

Static apnoea is not a competitive discipline – it is just trying to find something extreme. This is holding your breath and pre-oxygenising your body. The biggest problem is not the oxygen, the problem is the high levels of CO_2 in your body. You have oxygen for 40 minutes of breath in your body, but the problem is the higher levels of CO_2 that accumulate during your breath hold and you cannot expel them in any way. So you have to learn how to tolerate them. I was doing specific training for this: various forms of swimming and running without breathing – basically exercises to tolerate the levels of CO_2.

This discipline, it's not all mind, but mind has a lot to do with it. You have to stay calm and relaxed the whole time. You are suffocating and you need to breathe and in that process you need to be relaxed and enjoy the experience, even though it is not enjoyable at all. So it is a mind game. You need to control your body with your mind and be focused on what you're doing and never get discouraged with the fact that you need to breathe. My record is around 23 minutes. At around 11 or 12 minutes I need to breathe. Anything beyond that point is me trying to cheat my body.

We can split static into two phases. The first phase would be the easy phase. That is when you're floating, everything is cool. You don't need to breathe, everything is relaxed and fine. Then let's say, and it's different for everyone, around 50% of the way through your breaths, hold the involuntary diaphragm contractions start. You have these spasms around your tummy as your body tells you to inhale, but you're not inhaling – you're fighting the urge to breathe and prolonging your breath hold. The longer you go into your breath hold, the contractions start to be more frequent and much stronger. The levels of CO_2 are going up and the feeling is not pleasant. You're basically suffocating – you're drowning. But during your training when you get comfortable and familiar with the feeling and you know what is physiologically happening to your body, you just continue to do the breath hold. It's practice.

It's like running a marathon – the hardest period of your breath hold is not at the end, it's at 50-70% when it's already really hard but the end is still far away. Mentally, that is the hardest part. When you are around 21 minutes, then even though it's physiologically much harder, it's actually easier because you know that your goal is right there.

How I feel at the end depends on whether I succeeded or not. If I did well, then I am happy, but if not, then I am not. Physically, I am fine – after two or three breaths I am usually fine. It's like nothing happened.

In this discipline I do not think we are close to the maximum. For me, this 23 minutes was easier than I expected it to be. I think it can go much further. So theoretically I think people could go up to 30 minutes, but realistically I think it's going to be around 25-26 minutes. We will see.

Goran Čolak is a world record holding freediver.

Type Swimming
Date Year-round
Distance Varies
Main obstacles Hypothermia, death

Competitors say
It's a very condensed experience. I always compare it to running a marathon in 20 minutes rather than doing it in two hours.
Ram Barkai

Ice Swimming

Almost all of the challenges profiled in this book are selected because of the distance competitors travel while completing them. Ice swimming is different. The challenge does not manifest itself in the distance travelled. Rather, it comes from attempting to perform in adverse conditions and water that is cold enough, in extreme cases, to kill someone.

below In some ice swimming events the water freezes over before a swimmer completes a lap

Individuals have been ice swimming in various guises for centuries. In parts of Asia, the practice was closely tied to the celebration of religious festivals, while in Northern Europe swimmers have 'enjoyed' post-sauna ice baths for hundreds of years. More recently, ice swimming has developed into a competitive discipline in its own right. Events have been hosted around the globe, from London to Antarctica and South Africa to Siberia, with The International Ice Swimming Association overseeing these challenges and managing the records of those who complete them.

But like any extreme challenge, there are also those who choose to practise their art outside of the boundaries laid down by governing bodies. British swimmer Lewis Pugh became the first person to swim across the North Pole in 2007 (covering 0.62 miles/1km) in 18 minutes 50 seconds. To complete this challenge, which was done to highlight climate change, Pugh dived into water that was -1.8°C (28.7°F). At the other end of the globe, South African Ram Barkai earned a place in the Guinness Book of Records for the most southerly swim. Barkai completed a 0.62 mile (1km) swim in Queen Maud Land, Antarctica. The water temperature was 1°C (33.8°F).

Despite the relative freedom afforded to anyone who has set their own challenge, those attempting recognised ice swimming challenges generally abide by a set of 'rules' known as the English Channel Swimming Regulations. This means that a swimmer may only wear a standard swim costume (board shorts are permitted), swim hat, goggles, nose clip and ear plugs.

Ice swimming presents a unique challenge to the swimmer because of the natural reaction of the body to cold water. On a basic physiological level, as soon as a human enters cold water the body begins a process of 'shutting down'. Blood is pumped to the core, away from the limbs, to protect the vital organs. This poses significant problems for anyone aiming to perform athletically in water under 5°C/41°F – the temperature required for ice swimming. The combination of restricted blood flows with very cold temperatures can have a significant impact

to disorientation, this again impacts physical performance. Coordinating breathing patterns around the swim stroke becomes complicated as the athlete gasps for breath. To do so requires a level of calm and concentration that pushes the athlete through the various pain barriers they encounter.

Needless to say, those who compete in ice swimming events or challenges are physically prepared to do so. Ice swimming, or sudden immersion in near-freezing water, can kill somebody who is not prepared for the cold-shock reflex. Many ice swimmers will regularly immerse themselves in cold water so that their bodies become acclimatised to the impact of a swim. The body itself also begins to adapt. Studies have shown that ice swimmers often develop a layer of brown adipose tissue (fat) that enables them to generate more heat. Lewis Pugh, meanwhile, has been analysed by doctors who have found that he has developed a rare Pavlovian response to immersion in cold water whereby his

on physical performance. Studies have shown that swim efficiency and length of stroke are severely impacted, with complete swim failure an inevitable eventuality of prolonged exposure to this water.

Another natural physiological response to being plunged into cold water is to begin hyperventilating. As well as leading

left Most ice swimmers will attempt to cover 1km

below If prepared, the body adapts quickly and efficiently to immersion in cold water

core temperature increases in anticipation of a swim. As a result, the impact of the cold water on his body is reduced.

If the athlete is able to complete the challenge, the impact of the cold on the body continues following their exit from the water. As the blood rushes back to the non-essential organs, it draws the cold in towards the core. Heart rate patterns become disjointed and it is very easy for an athlete to be disorientated as hypothermia sets in. In short, both the act and process of recovery from an extreme cold swim places the human body under extreme levels of stress.

Ice swimming has become an increasingly popular pursuit over recent years. The willingness of a small number of individuals to attempt to perform in extremes of cold is not only an extreme physical challenge, but a potentially hazardous one too. However, with the right conditioning athletes are able to perform quite exceptional feats in some of the coldest places on earth. In so doing, they help to expand our knowledge of what the human body is capable of.

Ram Barkai

I live in Cape Town and the area of the Atlantic Ocean where we swim has a current that comes from Antarctica. That keeps the water temperature consistent during the year – it goes from 10°C to 15°C. Once you have adapted to that, you start asking 'how can I go colder?' The turning point was in February 2008 when I managed to get to Antarctica and do a record swim there. I did 1km in a frozen lake. The swim was a great experience. From there I started to explore and push to where we are now, which is just the beginning.

The most radical swim I've done was only a kilometre but it was in water temperature of 0°C in a frozen pool that they made in a lake in Siberia. The air temperature was -33°C. It was very radical being fully clothed and outdoors in the middle of the winter when there is no sun. Then you take off your clothes and dive in and swim a kilometre. By the time you do a length the water freezes on the way back. It's not dangerous in terms of swimming, but it's dangerous if you swallow it. It wasn't as difficult as I thought it would be because once in the water, as bizarre as it sounds, it was way warmer than the air. You obviously can't spend a lot of time in it, but there was a strange sensation of comfort.

It's a very condensed experience. I always compare it to running a marathon in 20 minutes rather than doing it in two hours. From the minute go, it is extreme. Because you are in such an extreme environment, you don't operate when panicking. You have to be very focused, calm and efficient – that is important. You are operating under a huge amount of pressure and stress. If you are not efficient with your energy, you will have to stop after a couple of minutes.

There is the usual shock of the body jumping into the water. You get used to it, and as you start swimming your body starts shutting down. Initially it is your hands, then the muscles get heavy because the body starts shutting down the blood supply to them. Towards the end of the swim the brain starts shutting down the supply of blood to your kidney and liver – obviously if you spend too much time in the water, the brain and the heart start competing – that's a risky area.

For me, the cold doesn't bother me so much when I get to the end of the swim (although I am very cold). What bothers me is that I am getting heavy in the water and so instead of being horizontal in the water my legs start to sink. The lower part of my body becomes a dead weight. Your muscles and your arms don't operate. You throw your arms at the water and they slip – they don't have enough power to grip the water. It's a common sight at the end of a cold water swim where someone can barely move – they are swimming but not covering any distance.

In your mind, from the beginning, you are very focused because the cold focuses you. You start getting heavier in your mind, and towards the end of the swim you start to lose control of it – this is a dangerous area. You can't really think straight, but you're still aware of what is going on. I always say that when you finish the swim you have to make sure you have enough to come back from it – the recovery is critical. It's not enough to have the energy to finish the distance; you've got to recover, and that is hard. It's risky because once you start warming up, your core body temperature plummets – it's a trip to hell and back.

Ram Barkai holds the world record for the most southerly swim. For more information, visit: www.internationaliceswimming.com.

Type Kayak
Date July – August
Distance 100 miles (160 km)
Main challenges Drowning, remoteness, rapids

Competitors say
In situations like that, you're more likely to get killed than hurt.
Eugene Buchanan

Kayak the Lower Bashkaus Gorge

The world's best kayakers scour the globe for the ultimate challenge. Some go in search of the biggest freefall, others look for first descents of challenging creeks or rivers. All, though, will at some point share the goal of signing their name in the Book of Legends that is nestled deep in the heart of the Lower Bashkaus Gorge.

right The Lower Bashkaus Gorge challenges the world's best kayakers

In 1975, Russian kayaker Igor Bazilevsky led a team onto Siberia's Bashkaus River. They were attempting to become the first kayakers to negotiate its Lower Gorge. Five of the team, including Bazilevsky himself, drowned during the expedition. One year later, the surviving members of that original team returned to the Bashkaus to complete what they had started. After successfully negotiating an extended stretch of Class V rapids, they stopped to build a monument to their fallen friends. This is where the Book of Legends now resides. Anyone who makes it through the Lower Gorge signs their name in this book, and cements their place in Bashkaus history.

Everything about kayaking the Bashkaus River is hard – even locating it. Nestled deep in the heart of Siberia (close to the Mongolian border), prospective paddlers face a multi-day journey just to reach one of the possible launch points for an expedition on the river. Those choosing a longer trip can launch from the village of Saratan, where after a short, punchy gorge the Bashkaus River flattens out until it reaches the town of Ulagan. Most attempting only the Lower Gorge will drive straight through Ulagan and try to negotiate the barely defined dirt roads that follow the river as it begins to cut a path through the hills around Tuskol. A campsite marks the beginning of the Lower Gorge, and this is where anyone who is not an exceptional waterman should be prepared to stop.

During the course of its journey from Saratan to Teletskoye Lake, the Bashkaus River drops nearly 8m (32ft)

for every mile. That is four-times the drop of the Colorado River that runs through the Grand Canyon. Most of that drop occurs in the Lower Gorge.

Those that paddle into the Lower Gorge are immediately sucked into a multi-day test of skill, strength and endurance. Within a few hundred metres of launching, they are thrown into a Class IV rapid (rated as advanced), immediately followed by a Class V (expert). After a brief portage and a section of flat river, the fun begins again with another run at a Class V rapid. And so it goes on. Over and over again the gorge throws up massive Class V and Class V+ rapids. Massive boulders line the route, churning up the water and creating all manner of dangers along the way. So much so that even the best kayakers repeatedly stop to recce the white water, and often choose to portage rapids that are simply too dangerous to tackle.

Safety is the primary consideration for those in the Gorge. Of course, a heavy collision with a submerged boulder can inflict painful injuries on a kayaker. However, such is the power of the water, coupled with the prevalence of the boulders, that the river contains numerous hidden hazards. Kayakers have to be particularly wary of siphons in this stretch of river – where the water flows through an opening beneath an obstacle like a boulder. If a kayaker gets dragged into a siphon, the kayak can easily become lodged underwater in a place where an exit is far from easy (or safe). If that happens and the kayaker does escape, they face an extended 'swim' down massive, dangerous rapids.

The Bashkaus River has earned a formidable reputation because of two things: the challenge of the river itself, and its spectacular remoteness. If anything goes wrong, there is no easy exit from the Lower Gorge. An expedition either has to float an injured teammate down the river, or climb them up and out of the Gorge. There is no foot route along this stretch of the Bashkaus, meaning that the only way out is to scale one of the surrounding cliffs. If a team is forced to retreat like this, once they have made it out of the Gorge, they

face a multi-day hike to civilisation through the Siberian wilderness.

Of course, knowledge of the river and technological advancements mean that these days an increasing number of those that find – and attempt – the Bashkaus get to sign their name in the Book of Legends. After they have done so, they continue on with their journey. It doesn't get easier though – anything but. A Class VI landslide rapid is the final sting in the tail of the river as the Lower Gorge levels out. It is one last brutal test for those that have pitted themselves against this most dangerous of rivers.

Eugene Buchanan

It's definitely one of the pinnacles of white water expedition boating. Just for the combination of its remoteness and its white water.

It has a 30 mile long lower canyon that is riddled with Class V rapids throughout. And it's very hard to get out of the canyon once you commit to it. So it's very much an all-or-nothing situation. It took us two weeks to get through that 30 miles. A self-support team of experienced boatmen could manage it in a couple of days, but we weren't in kayaks.

The reason it takes so long is that every time you come to a horizon line you have to get out and scout, decide if it's a safe enough rapid to run or not. If it is, you need to determine the safest line, set up safety, deal with any calamity that happens – swims and things. There are countless memorials attached to the walls there that remind you of people who have tried to run a lot of the rapids and died. That is always a grim reminder of what you are facing if things don't go according to plan.

The biggest challenge I faced was probably the portaging. It's very long and arduous, and it's time and calorie consuming. If you can run something safely, it's a lot more efficient than portaging all your gear around it. But if you don't run it safely … You've got to constantly weigh up those options: 'Can I get through this safely? If so, great. If not, what is worse? The swim or the portaging'. We were running low on food so were always weighing up those options.

I'm a lifelong kayaker, but when I went to the Bashkaus we were on homemade Russian catarafts. It's a different situation because on these catarafts there is no chance to roll – you're into the drink and at the mercy of the currents and have to rescue yourself. So I can only speak from that standpoint. You don't want to swim a Class V, but getting hurt there would be a big nightmare. The only way out is to float out with a busted leg. But in situations like that, you're more likely to get killed than hurt – you're more likely to drown than bust something up.

When we did it – which was 20 years ago – we flew to Moscow, took a three and a half day train ride, hired a bus to take us another 24 hours, from there we hired an army truck. We were with a Latvian team who were ready to hike in but we managed to wrangle a 4x4 who took us to the 'put in'. So it took us six days to reach that. Coming out, you float into a lake … Then you have to paddle across that whole lake, which if you're paddling is a two to three day proposition. We were able to catch the last ferry of the week – the next one wasn't coming for a week and we would have been stuck there. But luckily one of the guys was able to paddle across the lake and find a sailboat who gave us a ride.

Eugene Buchanan successfully signed his name in the Book of Legends in 1992. He wrote a book about the experience: Brothers on the Bashkaus.

Type Swim
Date May, June
Distance 3,716 miles (5,980km)
Main challenges Injury, conditions, wildlife

Competitors say
You feel very alone and very isolated. And you feel very small. You are just a little ant in this world. It's humbling.
Benoît Lecomte

Swim Across the Atlantic

Most people fly across it, some sail across it and a few even attempt to row it. But where there is water, there are swimmers, and the challenge of swimming across the Atlantic Ocean has consumed the minds and bodies of some of the world's strongest open water adventurers for years.

above Benoit Lecomte set out to swim from the USA to France in 1998

The second largest ocean in the world, the Atlantic separates North and South America on its west coast from Europe and Africa on its east. Between these two vast land masses lies a heaving expanse of water, occasionally punctuated by island groups such as the Azores. This ocean is the setting for perhaps the hardest open water swim that any human being has ever completed.

A swim crossing of the Atlantic has been attempted on numerous occasions, but completed (and verified) only once. Frenchman Benoît Lecomte took 73 days to finish the 3,716 mile (5,980 km) journey from Cape Cod in Massachusetts, USA, to Quiberon, France, in 1998. Lecomte swam for around eight hours per day, and was accompanied by a sailboat during the crossing. Some open water aficionados have questioned whether or not Lecomte travelled during his periods of rest on this boat (and so did not swim the entire distance of the crossing). He also received criticism for stopping in the Azores due to exhaustion. Regardless of these quibbles, Lecomte's swim was remarkable and he remains the only person to be widely credited with having swum across the Atlantic Ocean.

It goes without saying that swimming across the Atlantic is an immense physical undertaking. Training the body to be able to deal with prolonged exertion in – and exposure to – cold water takes months, if not years. But no amount of training can prepare an athlete for the rigours of swimming 8+ hours on back-to-back days for weeks on end. To that extent a swimmer will only find out whether their body is capable of completing a challenge of this magnitude once they have started it. One thing is, however, certain: the swimmer will experience severe cumulative fatigue during their attempt. This will not only affect their ability to continue swimming, but will also have an impact on their psychology.

In that respect, having the right mindset is essential. Of course, the ability to suffer is a given. The body will ache, salt sores will develop, and the mind must find a way to stay motivated despite the environment in which it is immersed. This environment is, for the most part, an unchanging, monotonous world devoid of sensory stimulation. The colour is blue, the hiss of the water in the ears is near-permanent, and the only view is the distant horizon. It is enough to break the mind of all but the toughest athletes.

Of course, there are days when the sea is not flat – anything but. However, those are the days that Atlantic swimmers plan to avoid. The window for crossing the ocean is relatively small, with most attempts being made in late spring/early summer. This is to avoid the start of the hurricane season. However, even without these super storms, the Atlantic is still capable of conjuring up wildly inclement weather. Swimmers who have attempted the crossing have reported swells in excessive of 20ft (6m), with some attempts having to be abandoned completely because of ferocious mid-Atlantic tempests.

Storms are not the only external variable that can impact the crossing. Large areas of the Atlantic are shark-prone, and every swimmer who has attempted the challenge has been forced to wear shark shields or do so in a shark cage. Jellyfish stings are another common threat to the comfort and safety of the swimmer. Of course, not all the wildlife is dangerous. Whales, dolphins and other creatures often pay visits to passing watercraft in the Atlantic. However, while they pose no direct threat to the swimmer, the shadows they cast through the deep blue sea can certainly toy with an exhausted mind.

Swimming across the Atlantic is a considerable logistical undertaking. Arranging support crews, boats and the pre-requisite safety equipment is an expensive challenge. What's more, with a limited window for favourable weather in the Atlantic of around seven weeks, everything has to fall perfectly into place for an attempt to stand any possibility of success.

Few challenges bring an athlete into such an isolated, uncontrollable environment as swimming across the Atlantic. It is extreme in every respect: from the sheer difficulty of completing the swim, to the environment in which the swimmer is immersed. That is perhaps why there has only been one verified crossing of this ocean. It is a truly epic challenge, and one that calls on every ounce of physical and mental strength the world's toughest swimmers can muster.

below It took Lecomte 73 days to complete the 3,716 mile journey

Benoît Lecomte

I like adventure. At the time I was training and knew a guy who rowed across the Atlantic and I was following him. I found out that he was rowing about the same pace as I was swimming, and so the idea of swimming across the ocean came up. I knew I needed a crew, a boat and so on, so it was a long process. After that, what really motivated me to go for it was that my father passed away from cancer and I wanted to do something in his memory.

As with anything like this, there are a lot of people who are physically better than me – I'm not Michael Phelps. But in anything like this, it is mind over matter. It is very repetitive, and doing it in a hostile environment needs strong determination. The mind makes the difference. When I was swimming I never thought about the entire distance, or how many miles I had to swim. I just focused on swimming one day at a time.

You feel very small – it puts everything in perspective. You are in the middle of the ocean and you don't see any reference points.

You're lacking most of the general stimulus that you have on land. It is very monotonous – the same thing over and over. And when you swim you have the same water rushing by your ears – that's the only sound you have. You have the same salty, heavy taste in your mouth. You are deprived of so many stimuli, and you have to rely on your mind not to get crazy. You feel very alone and very isolated. And you feel very small. You are just a little ant in this world. It's humbling.

I don't think there was one thing that was the hardest – it was an accumulation of things: the fact that you are isolated; that it was a difficult environment so that even if you are tired it is hard to sleep because of the motion of the boat; the same type of food; you cannot communicate with people that much – only the two crew members; the aching pains that you have every day. Mentally, it is very dragging. It's a long list of things that pile up on you that makes it very challenging.

I had a shark following me for five days. Every morning as I was getting ready the fin of the shark was going around the boat. And in the evening it was going around again. That was playing with my mind. We were using a device that created a magnetic field in the water. I was trying to stay as close as possible to that device. But the boat was sometimes pushed further away or faster so I couldn't always do that.

The shark wasn't the most difficult sea creature, though. The ones that caused me the most trouble were the jellyfish. For a couple of days I had to swim through millions of them – they were packed tightly together and I couldn't avoid them. Many got stuck between my snorkel and nose, and I got stung many times. I had to bite my tongue going through them as there was nothing I could do.

It was a bit surreal [to finish]. Everything comes at once – the people, being on land, the stimulus ... it's overwhelming. Even though I was very tired and wanted to sleep, I couldn't sleep at all because of all of those strong emotions. So in the middle of the night I went out on the street and had a walk just to enjoy it. It was raining and I remember enjoying the smells of the car exhausts. It was crazy.

Benoît Lecomte became the first person to swim across the Atlantic Ocean in 1998. He is now planning on swimming across the Pacific. For more information, visit: www.thelongestswim.com.

Type Row
Date Year-round
Distance Up to 10,000 miles (16093km)
Main challenges Weather, logistics

Competitors say
"The ocean is a dangerous place, but the Pacific really is much more hostile and intimidating than anywhere else."
Mick Dawson

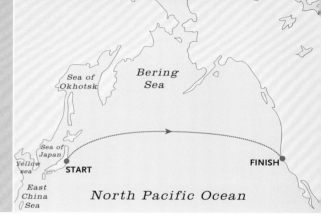

Row Across the Pacific

To row across the Pacific is to go head to head with the largest, most dangerous body of water on earth. Enormous waves and ferocious storms are common on this ocean, and being lost at sea is a very real possibility. What's more, the journey is long ... hundreds of days long. In short, it is the most extreme of ocean rows.

Ever since Ferdinand Magellan's crew was ravaged by war, disease and starvation during the first crossing of it, the Pacific Ocean has been both respected and feared by sailors in equal measure. Covering nearly one-third of the world's surface and stretching from the Arctic to the Southern Ocean, any crossing of the Pacific – whether from South America to Australia or Asia to North America – is a formidable undertaking. Even more so when you decide to row the thing.

Given that its waters lap the shores of so many continents, the trans-Pacific rower has plenty of routes to choose from. As such, there are plenty of 'firsts' in terms of expeditions. However, two in particular stand out. The first recorded crossing of the Pacific in a rowing boat was made by John Fairfax and Sylvia Cook in 1971/2. Over the course of 361 days they rowed 8,041 miles (12,941km) from San Francisco to Hayman Island (Queensland, Australia), making a number of stops along the way. Peter Bird is credited as being the first person to solo row the Pacific between 1982 and 1983, crossing 8,688 miles (13,982km) from San Francisco to the Great Barrier Reef in just 294 days (he was rescued by the Australian

Coast Guard at the Barrier Reef and so some dispute this record). Other great names of Pacific rowing who claim quite phenomenal firsts include Gerard d'Aboville and Jim Shekhdar.

Regardless of whether the crossing is made from Choshi (Japan) to Washington (USA) or from Lima (Peru) to the Marquesas Islands (French Polynesia), the challenges facing those that attempt to row the Pacific are enormous.

right Everything about a Pacific crossing is challenging

It goes without saying that the distances involved are phenomenal. Those attempting the Pacific will be forced to row almost non-stop for up to 20 hours per day. In so doing, estimates are that they will average 7,000 strokes for each 24 hour period, and will burn between 6,000 and 8,000 calories. It is a simply startling physical challenge that requires years of conditioning and preparation.

While the body can be trained, nothing can prepare a rower for the exhausting mental challenge that the Pacific affords them. Having the drive to row day after day, week after week, and month after month takes a unique breed of athlete. So does the ability to stay motivated in what can be an exceedingly monotonous environment. Pacific rowers often reflect upon weeks of toiling through a monochromatic world where there is little discernible difference between sea and sky. Passing ships are few and far between – and the giant tankers that appear on the horizon are just as likely to capsize the boat as they are to offer a greeting. Indeed, even sea life comes at a premium in vast swathes of this Ocean with dolphins, whales and sometimes the occasional disorientated fly making fleeting appearances. Being alone, or even with a companion, in an environment so devoid of sensory stimulation can push anyone to breaking point.

But for all the times the Pacific is flat and boring, there are times when it is quite the opposite: huge and dangerous. Storms and cyclones famously rip across the ocean, bringing with them winds of up to 75mph (120kph) and massive swells that can drag a boat hundreds of miles off course. These swells can easily reach 40ft (12m), throwing the relatively tiny boat between the peaks and troughs of an uncontrollable ocean. The sensation of being flung down the face of one of these massive waves has been likened to driving a car at speed into a brick wall. In these conditions, the boats regularly capsize (in most instances they will self-right), and can easily be damaged. Only the rower is in a position to right the boat and repair any significant damage, and they are often forced to do so while a storm rages around them.

Support crews do monitor the progress of trans-Pacific rowers, but help is often hundreds (if not thousands) of miles away. Indeed, the logistical planning and management of a Pacific Ocean row is almost as hard as the actual row itself. Given that most will attempt to complete the crossing

without stopping, rowers have to organise enough nutrition and hydration to cover them for a challenging eight-month expedition. Some choose to meet supply ships en route, while a select few aim to take everything they need with them. In this instance, calculations have to be nigh on perfect.

Successfully rowing the Pacific is an enormous challenge on every level. It requires mental and physical strength in abundance, not to mention the ability to manage both suffering and fear. The Pacific Ocean will test a rower to the extreme. Some never return from their voyage, others are lucky enough to make it through. All learn to appreciate the size and power of the mightiest ocean on earth.

top Pacific Ocean storms can be both frequent and violent

opposite There's little time for relaxation during a Pacific row

Mick Dawson

I think that until you've done it, whatever you assume – even having rowed across the Atlantic – is blown away by the reality of it. It is very different: another world. The word I used to describe it is 'industrial' on every level. The ocean is a dangerous place, but the Pacific really is much more hostile and intimidating than anywhere else.

It's the scale and intensity of it. As much as you get challenged on the Atlantic – and I've had dreadful days there – three or four times per day I've had total extremes on the North Pacific. Certainly, when Chris and I were successful – after five months at sea and heading into winter – that was the hardest thing I've ever had to do in my life. It was freezing cold, and the only heat on the boat was us. All of the clothing we had was worn out – we were in eight layers of clothing to keep warm – and everything just kept getting worse. The storms got longer and fiercer, the temperatures dropped and then we discovered the reality of rowing through Arctic currents coming down North America. At times we had to row backwards just to stay far enough North to get to San Francisco. It was epic – life or death really. We were really on the edge.

As a team that was probably the biggest achievement – that two blokes could put up with that situation (and each other) for all that time, and get through that and put the boat under the Golden Gate Bridge.

We rowed a routine of two on, two off around the clock. We rowed that routine religiously because we needed to be on the other side as soon as possible. Every hour that you are out there, something can go horribly wrong. And make no mistake, I loved being out there, but you have to go into it with the attitude that everything is about how fast you can get to the other side. We were talking about it and over the six months there were probably only 12 hours when we didn't row when we should have done – when we were slow getting out there after a storm and things like that.

Physically, I approached it as a sporting challenge. But there's so much more to it – it is 100% a mental test with physical elements. When you get to the start you're as fit as you can possibly be, but you're nothing like the person you need to be to get across the North Pacific. The only way to do that is to be on the North Pacific, rowing around the clock for weeks and months. There are all of the elements that go into that: you're absolutely destroyed by lack of sleep for 90% of the time; physically you deteriorate (we were 25kg + lighter when we finished); and the mental pressure is huge.

Mick Dawson and Chris Martin rowed the 7,000 miles from Choshi (Japan) to San Francisco (USA) in 189 days 10 hours and 55 minutes. For more information, visit: www.189days.com.

Type Swim
Date June – August
Distance Minimum 93 miles (150km)
Main challenges Sharks, Jellyfish, Currents

Competitors say
❝ *The jellyfish were hitting me and breaking apart and there was this intense pain. I was in so much pain I was screaming.* ❞
Chloe McCardel

Swim the Florida Straits

The waters of the Florida Straits attract swimmers from around the world. They come to bask in the temperate seas that lap against the white sand beaches. But every now and again they attract a swimmer with a different goal – one of the most challenging on the planet. That goal is to swim the Florida Straits, the body of water that separates Cuba from the USA.

above After multiple attempts, Diana Nyad finally completed the swim across the Florida Straits in 2013

Marathon swimming is a very particular sport. Athletes who attempt swims outside of organised competition are not bound by rules, but most choose to adhere to them. These rules are simple, and are known as the English Channel Swimming Association regulations (drawn up by the body that oversees attempts to swim across the English Channel). Under these regulations, the swimmer must start and finish any attempt on dry land. During the course of the swim they must not touch or rest on the boat that is supporting them. And they should only wear a swimsuit, goggles and swim hat. That is it.

But these regulations were designed for a particular challenge – the eponymous English Channel swim. As such,

they are not always appropriate for every swim challenge. Swimming the Florida Straits is probably one of them.

The Florida Straits is a relatively warm body of water that separates Cuba from the Florida Keys. Although a usually tranquil sea, this strait is the origin for the Gulf Stream, a temperate current that flows across the Atlantic and influences climates as far afield as Newfoundland and Northern Europe. This current has a profound impact on anyone attempting to cross the Straits. First and foremost, it is unpredictable, and changes both its speed and direction with surprising regularity. These changes impact the navigation of the swimmer, who can easily find themselves being dragged far off-course. They can also lead to changeable weather conditions, with the Gulf Stream occasionally whipping up strong winds and ocean swells.

But the Gulf Stream is not a reason to question the suitability of English Channel regulations in this swim. Rather, it is what lies beneath the Straits that necessitate that. During the course of the crossing the swimmer will pass through a variety of 'zones' all of which harbour a variety of sharks and jellyfish. The former are common in the waters around Florida, with tiger, bull, hammerhead and white tip sharks – all known man-eaters – regularly spotted in the area. In fact, they pose enough of a threat that only one attempt on the Straits has ever been made without shark protection – by Chloe McCardel in 2013.

The prevalence of box jellyfish arguably poses a far greater threat to the safety of the swimmer. This jellyfish

– more commonly associated with the waters of the South Pacific – is responsible for more deaths than any other ocean creature. For reasons hitherto unknown, it is now an increasingly common inhabitant in the Florida Straits. Their incredibly painful stings can result in cardiac arrest, cerebral haemorrhage and death if not treated immediately.

During her much-publicised crossing of the Straits in 2013, Diana Nyad used a variety of means to negate these threats. The support kayaks that accompanied her carried shark deterrents, and she swam in a specially made (non-buoyant) body suit that protected her against stings. She also wore gloves, booties and a silicone mask with a retainer to ensure no part of her body was exposed during the attempt. Finally, a specially designed 'lane line' was attached to the main boat and allowed her to follow a route through the water.

Nyad was the third person to swim across the Florida Straits, and was the first to do so without a shark cage. In 1978, Walter Poensich made the crossing using a shark cage and fins (he also took a couple of rest stops on the support boat). Meanwhile, Australian Susie Maroney completed a non-stop swim across the Straits in a shark cage in 1997

(she has also completed swims from both Jamaica and Mexico to Cuba). In 2013, Chloe McCardle attempted to become the first person to swim the Straits under English Channel regulations, but was forced to abort her attempt after 11 hours because of jellyfish attacks.

Regardless of the 'tools' utilised in an attempt on the Florida Straits, it remains an enormous physical undertaking. The distances involved mean that the swimmer can easily expect upwards of 48 hours in the water without a break. To put that in perspective, Diana Nyad became only the twelfth person in recorded history to swim for that length of time. The pressure this places on the body is extreme, with shoulder injuries and severe fatigue an inevitable consequence of the challenge.

Every variable involved in the Florida Straits swim challenges the world's strongest open water swimmers. From strong currents that can easily drag a swimmer off course to the very real threat of marine wildlife that are more than capable of causing, at best, extreme pain. It is a truly formidable challenge that only the strongest, toughest swimmers are able to conquer.

Chloe McCardel

I wanted to do it because nobody has crossed it in traditional marathon swimming rules – using caps and goggles. When I attempted it, the only people who had crossed it did it in a shark cage, in flippers ... it's a very different swim if you have external aides assisting you.

I had a brainstorm about the major challenges of the swim. First of all, there is the distance – 170km is a long way. The English Channel, which is the pinnacle of marathon swimming, is 34km. So it's out of the league of nearly everyone. Then there is the box jellyfish, which can be extremely challenging. Diana Nyad got stung by a few of them on multiple attempts by the sound of it. Then there is the Gulf Stream. It's not like you're swimming through a normal stretch of water. You've got to try and navigate a really difficult, strong patch of water that can move up to 9kph. It's not taking you to the US (everyone starts from Cuba) and you have to get across it. The approval process is extremely difficult because the US and Cuba don't have official relationships. We had to get a huge amount of permissions and licenses to get the crew – so the financial and time cost is enormous. There also isn't a wealth of knowledge of that particular waterway. So on multiple levels, it's a very difficult swim.

I chose to do it under traditional rules. They are self-imposed – people can choose whatever type they like. So I swam with no cage and no flippers. Unlike Diana Nyad I had no face shield, nobody touching me, I just had basic Speedos ... I did it very traditionally and had recognised observers. You can do these one-off swims in any way you like. I just happened to set the bar quite high for my attempt – maybe that was my downfall. I like to set a standard that is scrutinised by others.

I swam for eleven hours so can only talk about it from that perspective. The conditions I had were very flat – the wave height was close to nil. We didn't have any issues with sharks. In many ways it was looking like a great day for a swim. But when we entered the Gulf Stream it was going North East and taking me away from my finish point. I had to swim strongly to fight that, otherwise I would be swimming to Mexico. I kept fighting as I knew that eventually I would pop out of it. That was quite difficult.

I was feeling content, but then as soon as the sun went down this blanket of jellyfish rose up to the surface. I had seen a few hanging about, but they just lifted. They were hitting me and

breaking apart and there was this intense pain. I was in so much pain I was screaming. I had shark divers dragging me out because I couldn't swim and they were getting stung. These jellyfish were everywhere. All the information we had from locals was that the jellyfish weren't around at that time of year.

I won't go back. The conditions are too unpredictable and I don't want to lower my standards. My standards are bathers, goggles and cap. I don't believe in wetsuits, face masks. When does it stop becoming swimming and start becoming surfing? As the standards I set for myself, it's not a plausible swim until the jellyfish situation changes. And it may not change, it may get worse.

Chloe McCardel has completed two double crossings of the English Channel and now coaches those attempting the crossing (solo or in a relay). For more information, visit: www.chloemccardel.com.

ON TWO
FEET

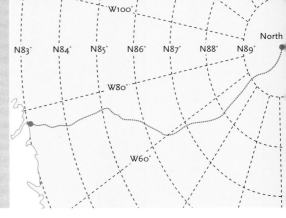

Type Trek
Date February – May
Distance circa 500 miles (800km)
Main challenges Cold, Terrain

Competitors say
The North Pole is easily ten times harder than Everest or the South Pole.
Eric Larsen

Trek to the North Pole

Constantly moving, constantly breaking, constantly rising and falling, the ice that sits above the Arctic Ocean is a temperamental floe. Some years it offers safe passage to those attempting to reach the North Pole, other years it does not. Every year, however, it provides a unique challenge that tests the mettle of the world's toughest Polar explorers.

Like many 'extreme' challenges, there are relatively easy ways of getting to the North Pole. In fact, every year plenty of people do it without really breaking a sweat. Some fly there, others are dropped off and walk the last few miles as part of a fully supported tour operation, while a select few choose to run a marathon across it. But those kind of trips are for tourists. The adventurers who want to properly challenge themselves against the Arctic start long before the ice floe gets its hands on them. They start on solid ground.

Unlike the South Pole, which is situated on a landmass (Antarctica), the geographic North Pole is covered by 4,261m (13,980ft) of water. Usually one metres (3ft) of ice sits on top of this water, and the Pole remains almost permanently frozen (although recently open water has been spotted there).

Because it sits on top of the Arctic Ocean, the Polar ice pack is in constant motion. For the most part it travels in an Easterly direction, depositing ice into the North Atlantic. This poses a constant problem for those attempting to reach the North Pole from the two most common expedition launch points: Canada's Ellesmere Island or Russia's Cape Arktichevsky. Expeditions that set out from either base find that as soon as they set foot on the floe, they are being carried away from their goal. This 'conveyor belt' effect means that simply making progress towards the Pole is a constant battle. What's more, any periods spent resting on the ice invariably find expeditions being carried further south.

An additional consequence of the perpetual motion of

this ice is that the floe on which the adventurers are crossing is always changing. This can impact the ice in two ways. First, it can open up leads within the floe. These are channels of open water that the adventurers either have to cross (by swimming or using their pulk as a raft), or by walking around – which can be a significant diversion depending on the size of the lead. Just as the ice can crack and break, so too can it rise to form massive pressure ridges. These ridges can be metres high and often look like someone has thrown giant blocks of ice across the floe. Sometimes these ridges are isolated, at other times expeditions have to negotiate mile upon mile of broken blocks of ice. Doing so is slow, back-breaking work, particularly when hauling heavily-laden pulks.

Any expedition attempting an unsupported trek to the North Pole has to carry with them everything that they need to survive for up to two months on the ice. In these conditions, where help is often days away, any oversight can be deadly. As such, many expeditions take pulks weighing up to 150kg (330lbs) with them. While these pulks are designed for polar travel, it can still be difficult to drag them across fractured ice floes. Pressure ridges sometimes form insurmountable barriers, while soft, thick snow makes pulk dragging an exhausting process. Conditions on the ice can be so bad that at times expeditions have to relay their equipment, so making multiple trips back and forth to cover short distances.

The physical challenges of a trip to the North Pole are merely exacerbated by the harsh weather conditions that expeditions can expect in the Arctic. Temperatures can fall as low as -50°C (-58°F) and the humidity levels are high. Storms pose a very real threat, and can blow with enough ferocity to leave adventurers trapped in their tents for days. These storms shift and break the ice, and can even reverse the movement of the entire Arctic ice pack.

All of these challenges are set against a background of a ticking clock. Expeditions can only carry a finite amount of supplies, and so must manage their progress and equipment based on tight timeframes. Not doing so not only condemns the expedition to failure, but can be – and sometimes is – deadly. The pressure is immense.

While many make the trip to the North Pole every year, few are willing or able to tackle an unsupported, unassisted journey across the ice. It is an expedition that calls on every ounce of an adventurer's physical and mental strength. It pits them against the best and the worst of one of the most hostile areas on the planet. And it does so in an environment that is moving and changing beneath their feet. In short, it is a truly extreme challenge and one that only accomplished polar adventurers dare tackle.

Eric Larsen

I call the North Pole expedition one of the most difficult on the planet. It's an environment that so few people understand. You're travelling across ice that is floating on water so it is moving. It's not very thick either – maybe a metre and a half at its thickest point, and sometimes it's a few centimetres thick. It's broken into sheets, and these can be several kilometres wide or a few metres across. And they are in constant motion depending on the wind, the tide and the ocean current. So these sheets can crack apart and form an open section of water – which you have to get across somehow. Or they can collide together and form a pressure ridge, which can be blocks of ice the size of a house that stretch on for miles and can be 10 metres high. It's a very dynamic surface that is constantly changing.

That in itself probably isn't that difficult, but you're also dealing with -40°C temperatures. It's very humid. Unlike Antarctica which is a desert, the Arctic Ocean is humid and that affects your ability to stay safe and not get icy.

Then there's an overall drift to the ice. It's not only moving around and breaking, but the overall drift is to the South, so it's like you're on a conveyer belt. You set up your tent at night and you're losing distance – up to 2 or 3 miles.

For the first three weeks of the trip, the ice is moving and it's hitting Canada – that's the roughest. It's all pressure, there are no clear routes. Our sleds weigh 300 pounds on day one and we can't pull them singularly so we're relaying them. That means for every mile we go we travel three. For the first three weeks we average two-and-a-half miles per day. If we had continued at that rate, we would have needed 129 days. But we've got 50 days of food and fuel, so now we're in a situation where our sleds are a little lighter, but we're only 50 miles from the start and have a huge gap to go.

The problem is that now the snow is soft and slow and it's like we're dragging anchors through it. Then we get to the point where we have 10 days of supplies and 180 miles to go. What do we do? We cut our sleep and we're travelling 15 hours per day. Then we're 50 miles from the Pole and all hell breaks loose because there's water everywhere. It's unrelenting. That's compounded by the fact the difficulty level is increasing, and your physical and mental level to cope with it is decreasing. Now you're at this point where it's a perfect storm of crap.

At the South Pole, there is a marker. At the North Pole, there's nobody there. And that ice is moving. So that ice is not going to be the North Pole in five seconds. And it looks like everything else. The only positive aspect is that we don't have to put ourselves in danger. It's an end of the suffering – that's the joy.

Eric Larsen is a Polar explorer who has completed multiple expeditions in the Arctic, Antarctic and Himalayas. For more information, visit: www.ericlarsenexplore.com.

Type Walk
Date Year-round
Distance circa 4,250 miles (6,839km)
Main challenges War, infection, fatigue

Competitors say
❝I had to wade through marshes, hack through jungles, or walk across soft sand dunes next to the river.❞
Levison Wood

Walk the Length of the Nile

Snaking its way through eleven countries, the Nile is not only a source of life for millions of Africans, but has been a source of inspiration for explorers and geographers for centuries. A few have managed to paddle the length of this mighty river, but nobody has been able to walk it. Until now ...

below Levison Wood spent more than nine months walking the length of the Nile

Finding the source of the River Nile has fascinated some of the greatest minds in history. Alexander the Great searched for it, as did the Romans. The quest to locate its origin made household names out of Victorian explorers like David Livingstone, Henry Morton Stanley, John Speke and Richard Burton. Even today, geographers still debate its true source, although most accept that it starts life as a small, muddy stream in the Nyungwe Forest of Rwanda. The water that

bubbles out of the ground in this forest begins a 4,250 mile (6,839km) journey to the Mediterranean Sea.

This source was the point where, in 2013, Levison Wood began his quest to become the first person to walk the length

of the River Nile. A number of explorers have, throughout history, travelled the length of the Nile by boat. However, nobody had ever managed to do so on foot alone. It was an extraordinary expedition that would eventually travel through six countries, across a variety of terrain and numerous ecosystems.

From the cool upper reaches of the Rwandan mountains to the dry expanse of the Sahara Desert (by way of the world's largest swamp), Wood was forced to deal with extremes of conditions during his expedition. The Sahara, in particular, posed a significant barrier to completing his trek. Wood hit the desert at the beginning of the summer, and was forced to walk through its often soft sands in temperatures pushing 55°C (131°F). Physical performance for anyone in this kind of relentless heat is tough. But keeping going in an environment where food and water can be scarce is also dangerous. Indeed, the heat on certain stretches of the journey (not just the Sahara) was so severe that one experienced outdoor journalist who had joined up with the expedition to write about it died after three days of trekking.

Wood arrived at the Sahara in the summer because of the need to avoid an even more formidable barrier on the upper reaches of the river: The Sudd Swamp. People have been known to simply disappear in this swamp, which can grow to more than 93,000 square miles (150,000km²) during the wet season. It is just one of many difficult stretches on the upper reaches of the river. Coming out of the mountains, the Nile passes through thick jungle, marshes and a number of large areas of swampland. Negotiating any of these environments is physically and mentally hard work. Trails have to be cut and paths found both on dry land and through water that is often knee or waist deep.

These environments are home to one of the other great challenges of an expedition along the Nile: the wildlife. From source to sea, any expedition along the Nile will cross through the habitats of wildlife that is genuinely dangerous. Lions, crocodiles and hippos are all regularly spotted in places like Uganda and Tanzania. More dangerous than the game animals, though, are the mosquitos. The river is not only a natural home to these insects, but winds its way through many high-risk malarial zones.

In fact, the only thing more deadly than mosquitos on this expedition is other people. Historical expeditions frequently related stories about warring tribes, desert bandits or aggressive locals. While things have undoubtedly changed in the area, many problems still persist. During his recent expedition, Wood was mugged, had to deal with corrupt local

above Wood was forced to find paths along the river as it snaked its way through forests, swamps and the Sahara

officials and pass through some areas that were, quite simply, dangerous. At one stage he was forced to abandon 400 miles (643km) of his journey due to civil war in South Sudan (he plans on returning to walk this part of the Nile once the war is finished). Of course, the people who cause these problems are a minority along the river. However, the danger they pose is real, and the ability to disrupt an expedition is profound.

Overcoming these numerous challenges requires a mental fortitude beyond many individuals. Coupled with the very real threats that plague a trip along the Nile is the fact that it is an almost overwhelmingly long expedition. Wood covered upwards of 25 miles (40km) per day with one rest day every two weeks. Being able to stay motivated and keep walking these distances for more than nine months demands a singular mindset and impressive levels of determination.

To walk the Nile is to follow in the footsteps of the world's greatest explorers. It is to disappear into the heart of a vast continent and confront a series of truly formidable challenges. To be successful requires supreme levels of mental and physical fortitude, plus a healthy dose of luck. Perhaps that is why nobody – as yet – has been able to complete this trek in full.

Levison Wood

I've always had a passion for Africa, and for the Nile in particular. I've been leading expeditions around the world for a while and I thought I would give it a go – nobody had ever done it.

It was the hardest thing I've ever done. I've walked across Madagascar, trekked across Afghanistan and Iraq; I've been to about 80 countries. This was the hardest physically and mentally. I was up against every kind of terrain, from mountains in Rwanda to swamp lands, savannah and the entire Sahara Desert in the summer. It was tough.

There was a lot of danger. You've got the risk from the wildlife – you have every kind of predator in Africa, especially when you're camping by the river. I was walking through national parks where you have elephants, lions, hippos and crocodiles – not to mention snakes and scorpions. You also have medical threats – malaria is always there and you're getting bitten on a daily basis.

The threat from people is more predictable. Ninety-nine per cent of the people were brilliant, but you meet a few bad eggs anywhere you go. I was mugged a couple of times, questioned by police, arrested more times than I can remember. And politics of war got in the way. A civil war kicked off in South Sudan two weeks after I set off and that meant I had to skip over a small portion of the trip – I couldn't walk through the Sudd Swamp because of it. I was booted out of the country and had to start again North of the border. I hope I can go back and complete the trek. I knew there would be risks, but there was a lot of stuff on an expedition that you can't prepare for.

Physically, the biggest challenge was crossing the Sahara in the summer. The temperatures were incredible (50-55°C) and you have to be really careful about not pushing yourself too hard. I lost a journalist – he died after three days because of the heat. That reinforces the fact the dangers are real and you have to be careful. Unless you're aware of the signs when your body is starting to pack in, then it's easy to succumb to the heat or dehydration.

I walked through six different countries. In the North, through Egypt, it's obviously very populated so it's quite easy. You have roads and villages and that's fairly straightforward. In the jungle – and three-quarters of it are jungle – you have some very wild places. And you have the world's biggest swamp, the Sudd Swamp. The river just turns into a swamp the size of England and you have to walk around it. In Rwanda it goes through rainforest and the river goes underground for part of it. My ambition was to stay as close to the river as possible, where possible. Sometimes that meant I had to wade through marshes, hack through jungles, or walk across soft sand dunes next to the river in Sudan.

Once you get past the halfway mark your eyes are on the prize. I had all of these romantic notions of what the Mediterranean Sea would look like but, to be honest, it was the opposite. Where the river meets the sea it's a military no-go zone. It was a bit of an anti-climax. But it was good to finish and have achieved something. It will certainly stay with me for the rest of my life.

Levison Wood completed his expedition along the Nile in 2014. For more information, visit: www.levisonwood.com.

Type Run
Date Year-round
Distance 350 miles (563km)
Main challenges Sleep deprivation, conditions

Competitors say
❝I was running along, falling asleep and continuing to keep my legs turning over.❞
Dean Karnazes

North America
South America
Europe
Africa
Asia
Australia
Antarctica

Complete a Multi-Day Non-Stop Run

The world's best ultra runners are capable of some quite considerable feats of endurance. Whether they decide to run around the world, or to 'simply' run 5,649 laps of a single block in New York City, many complete challenges that are far beyond the capabilities of 'normal' people. There is one run, however, that has no finish line. Rather, that finish line comes when the athlete simply says 'enough'. That is the challenge of non-stop running.

right Dean Karnazes ran for 350 miles without stopping

Running non-stop is a relatively simple concept. Athletes begin their run at a pre-defined point and follow a course that they have agreed with their race 'crew' (who are also on hand to help manage nutrition, hydration and safety). From the moment they begin the run, the athlete basically does not stop. That means no stopping to eat, limited toilet breaks, and absolutely no stopping for sleep. Usually, during the course of a race, athletes will pause to change worn-through socks and shoes, but that is it. It really is a brutal test of an individual's physical and mental strength.

World-famous ultra runner Dean Karnazes holds the record for the longest non-stop run. In 2006, Karnazes ran 350 miles (563km) in 80 hours and 44 minutes (or three and a half days). During the run his average speed was 13 minutes per mile. American Pam Reed is credited with being the first person to run 300 miles (482km) non-stop, while New Zealand athlete Kim Allan ran and walked 310 miles (498km) over the course of 86 hours 11 minutes and 9 seconds in 2012.

It goes without saying that attempting to run any distance continuously over a number of days is an immense physical undertaking. Not only does it place the body under enormous pressure, but can very easily lead to complete physical breakdown. Bones, muscles, the back and the neck are all placed under considerable strain. The feet, too, take a beating, with athletes forced to keep on running despite losing toenails or suffering the inevitable blistering that is

part and parcel of so many hours spent pounding the road.

The body suffers internally, too. Immune systems weaken as muscles and cells are given scant time to recover. At the same time, the sustained lack of 'regular' nutrition and hydration during the challenge merely exacerbates the negative effects of the run itself. In many respects, the body starts to battle with itself – with internal systems struggling to cope with the pressure that they are under. Following his successful attempt at completing 350 miles non-stop, Karnazes suffered from hypothermia.

Another reason behind this physical breakdown is the lack of sleep that runners subject their bodies to. Sleep deprivation is often cited as the hardest part of this challenge, with athletes suffering from hallucinations on the road. While this undoubtedly impacts the athletes' ability to realise their goals, it also brings with it very real safety implications. Most non-stop running challenges take place on open roads. When an athlete becomes disorientated or begins to hallucinate they can easily lose their balance and weave out into the path of oncoming vehicles. Of course, support cars are there to

ensure their safety, but they cannot guarantee the athlete will not stumble at an inopportune moment.

Overcoming the challenges associated with a non-stop run requires considerable mental strength. Pain, coupled with sleep deprivation, is an inevitable part of this challenge, and managing the body's response to it is essential. So, too, is the ability to manage the mind in the face of a quite overwhelming objective. Running for 24 hours non-stop is hard enough. Knowing that that timeframe is just one-third – perhaps even less – of your target distance is too much for many people to process. Doing so is the key to staying motivated.

Over the years, many ultra runners have challenged themselves in races with no fixed end point. On the track, legendary athletes like Yiannis Kouros have run upwards of 188.6 miles (303.5km) during a 24-hour meet. Meanwhile, records for treadmill running are equally as impressive, with Ireland's Tony Mangan covering 251.79 miles (405.22km) in 2008. However, while these races boast no absolute finish line, they do have a set cut-off point. What's more, athletes have the option of resting during the event (although most choose not to). A non-stop run has no cut offs. It continues for as long and as far as the athlete is physically capable. As such, it is a supreme battle between the mind and the body. And when the body does eventually win that battle, the athlete has little choice but to collapse.

Dean Karnazes

I had originally set my sights on a 500-mile run. I was never ultimately able to do what I wanted to do. I don't want to say that what I did was reaching my goal; it was a shortened distance.

I can go through one night without sleep just fine. A second night without sleep, you just fade in and out and are a little less lucid. But I tell you: that third night without sleep was a new experience for me. I found myself sleeping on the run at multiple points. The first time it happened I couldn't figure out what had happened – I found myself running down the middle of the road, and I thought 'why am I running in the middle of the road? I know better than that'. So I meandered back to the side of the road, and then it happened again. I woke up and I was running down the middle of the road and I realised that I was sleep running. I was just running along, falling asleep and continuing to keep my legs turning over. That was a unique experience!

The body is amazing. At points you feel pretty good. Even towards the end of the 350 miles. There were points where I thought 'I can keep going'. I felt strong. There might be a mile or two section where the pain subsides and the muscle ache goes away. But then in the span of 20 steps you can go from feeling really good to feeling like you've just been run over by a truck. The body starts going in and out of these cycles: rejuvenation to deterioration. These cycles get more and more pronounced – the highs get a little bit higher and the lows get deeper. And that starts happening with greater frequency the further you progress.

On this endeavour I was being followed by a media crew and there was a helicopter filming from above. I'll never forget it; it was about mile 315 and I was running along and I started having these visions of looking down upon a guy who was running – like I was in the helicopter or a bird. And then I realised 'oh my god, that's me!' I'm not really a spiritual guy, but that was close to an out-of-body experience as anything I have ever felt. My head was not in my body as I was running along. That was kind of trippy.

When I hit the 350 mile mark at about 10 p.m., the heat of the day had left me so overheated – my muscles were so hot – that all I was running in was a pair of shorts. I had a sip of champagne and it occurred to me that everyone had big jackets on. And then it popped into my head that it was cold – within 20 seconds I had hypothermia. They put me in a mummy bag and all that was exposed was my face. I just remember laying on my back saying, 'I'm hungry'. They were spooning something into my mouth and then the next thing I knew I woke up the next morning.

In theory, if you could learn how to sleep while you were running, I think a human could make it to 500 miles. The problem is the faster you go to minimise the number of nights you're running, your body breaks down. The slower you go, the more sleep deprivation you face. I really think that someone could do it ... but I'm not that person. I mean, 350 miles? I was done at that point.

Dean Karnazes is a world-famous ultra marathon runner. For more information, visit: www.ultramarathonman.com.

Type Trek
Date Year-round
Distance circa 4,500 miles (7,200km)
Main challenges Heat, dehydration, orientation

Competitors say
I could travel day after day, week after week and month after month and never come across a river, a road or a city.
Michael Asher

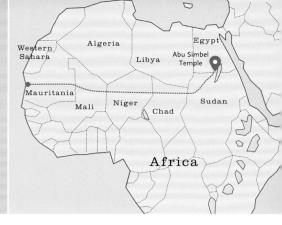

Trek Across the Sahara

For centuries, the Sahara Desert has captured the imaginations of adventurers and armchair enthusiasts alike. But a desert that once presented a near impenetrable barrier to Central Africa is now, for many, a playground. On its fringes athletes run 'across' it, enthusiasts drive cars through it, and those looking to follow in the footsteps of Lawrence of Arabia take camel tours deep into the interior. But the Sahara is massive. And to truly explore this sea of sand is to tackle one of the remotest, bleakest parts of the globe. It is to pit the human body against extremes of weather, attrition and sensory stimulation.

Human beings have been exploring the Sahara for millennia. Greek historian Herodotus referred to sub-Saharan Africa in writings dating back to 480BC, while fabled explorer Ibn Battuta (1304-1369) crossed parts of the desert during his well-documented travels in Africa and Asia. But exploration in the region increased dramatically when Europe – obsessed by the prospect of colonisation – took an interest. Many famous explorers attempted the crossing, and many disappeared in this sea of sand. But as knowledge of the region, its oases and, most importantly, its people improved, explorers slowly but surely managed to forge a path through the desert.

On paper, the Sahara today is nowhere near the impenetrable barrier to Central Africa that it once was. The Trans-Saharan Highway dissects the heart of the desert, and satellite imagery has unlocked its hidden interior. But that is on paper.

In reality, the Sahara continues to pose a considerable challenge to those planning an expedition into its interior. Indeed, that challenge is so formidable that, even with advancements in technology and engineering, only a handful of expeditions have managed to cross the desert in its

left The lonely path through the Sahara Desert can play tricks with the mind

entirety. What's more, those that do are forced to employ the same techniques that served early European explorers relatively well: they travel on foot and by camel.

In the middle of the Sahara, the success or failure of an expedition is dependent upon an intricate knowledge of the region itself. For that purpose, many expeditions employ Tuareg guides. The paths the Tuareg tread – which are often hundreds of years old – lead from oasis to oasis, providing humans and their camels with access to water and sometimes food. However these oases do sometimes dry up, and expeditions can be forced to walk for multiple days without finding even brackish water.

Even if an expedition is able to access basic nutrition and hydration supplies, desert travel is tough. Temperatures in the Sahara regularly swing between extreme highs of up to 58°C (136°F), and nighttime lows that plunge below 0°C (32°F). As such, many expeditions travel through the early morning and late afternoon, resting during the hottest part of the day. As well as extreme temperatures, sandstorms are a common desert phenomenon. Fierce winds whip the sand through the sky, reducing visibility to a matter of metres and making it nigh on impossible to continue. For the Tuareg, who navigate by the stars, extended sandstorms can be fatal.

Although the margin between life and death in the Sahara is small, the distances are massive. Help can sometimes be hundreds of miles away, and the goal of the expedition can quite easily be thousands of miles 'down the road'. Thousands of miles equates to hundreds of days of tough desert travel. Having the mental fortitude to manage so many days in the relentless heat of this sea of sand is beyond many individuals.

Despite all of the challenges, individuals and expeditions do manage to make it across the Sahara. In 1986, Michael Asher and Mariantoinetta Peru became the first recorded

below A sea of sand, the Tuareg still find their way across the desert using the stars

expedition to cross the desert from the Atlantic (Nouakchott, Mauretania) to the Nile (Abu Simbel, Egypt) by foot and camel. More popular is one of the North to South routes through the Sahara, although popularity is relative in this region of the world.

Crossing the Sahara – whether from North to South or West to East – is a formidable challenge. A true wilderness, and one of the few places on earth where camels are a preferred form of transport over vehicles, the Sahara is a land of extremes. To successfully cross it is to challenge the body and mind on every level. And it is to call upon the knowledge and experience of those who have walked this desert for centuries, and know the secrets to surviving it.

Michael Asher

I went to work in the Sudan as a volunteer teacher and my school was on the edge of the Sahara. I was entranced by the landscape – it was like standing on the shore of this vast sea that went on and on. And it was wild. What struck me was the idea that if I set off in a straight line from that place I could travel day after day, week after week and month after month and never come across a river, a road or a city until I reached the Atlantic – 3,000 miles away. That's when I first had this idea and I discovered that there was no record of it having been done. It was quite a few years before it came about.

I went to live with a nomad tribe. I became one of them. I lived with them, I dressed like they did, I learned to speak Arabic fluently. I spent three years with them and travelled thousands of miles by camel, so I knew the desert and knew camels pretty well by then. After I left them, I decided to try this crossing, but then I met my wife and we decided to do it together.

The conditions are the hardest thing. It's not just like walking across a place on a sunny day. We started in August and it was very hot – we recorded temperatures up to 52°C. There are the winds, and we went through a sandstorm that blew for a week. The locals can't navigate in sandstorms, but we had a compass. Nomads go to ground in a sandstorm and they die of thirst. That's strangely pretty common for nomads.

There were also political problems. As we crossed the border between Mali and Niger – of course there are no borders, it's just the desert – we came across a nomad group. They were very friendly, as they always are, and they invited us to stay the night. But when we woke up the camp was surrounded by police and we were arrested and held in the nearest town for six days. Eventually the permission came through. We had quite a few experiences like that; we were arrested twice in Chad.

The scariest thing that happened was on the last leg of the journey in Sudan. There were just the two of us – we had no guide – and we had been travelling for days, and we started to lose touch with reality. We had travelled thousands of miles and we started hearing voices in the night, seeing eyes and hearing people walking behind us. Both of us had this experience and we were 200 miles from the nearest settlement – there was nobody. That was worrying because when we arrived in a nomad camp that rescinded. I don't know why it happened.

We were very tired and after going 10 days with no people and no signs of people – no tracks or animal droppings – it was that fear of loneliness.

Water is hard to find. We did have maps. But some of the maps aren't really accurate – so some of the wells aren't there, for example. Even the guides struggle. At the start in Mauritania, we had gone for days without seeing anybody and the guide told us there was a well tomorrow. We were already thirsty and the next day came and we didn't find the well. The guide said, 'It's okay, we'll find one tomorrow,' but we were really thirsty. We did find one the next day but there was no water. That was a problem. The following day we found these small melons that grow in the Sahara and we collected dozens of them; these saved our lives.

When you get close to nature, you get drawn into it. The rhythm of our nature was all about finding water, finding food and grazing for our camels. We felt so close to nature that when we got to civilisation, it appeared really ugly. We didn't want to go back.

Michael Asher and his wife, Mariantoinetta, completed the first west-to-east crossing of the Sahara in 1984. For more information, visit: www.deep-ecology.com.

Type Run
Date April – November
Distance circa 3,118 miles (5,017km)
Main challenges Terrain, conditions, injury

Competitors say
Every morning I put my hands on my stroller and just kept on running. That was it. I just kept on running.
Björn Suneson

Run Across America

The road across North America is long. It is undulating. And at times it is filled with potholes, pitfalls and perilous volumes of traffic. But the challenge of running across the USA has inspired many, forcing them to face up to one of the most challenging runs on the planet.

below Björn Suneson has run across America on four occasions

At 3:30 p.m. on March 4th 1928, 199 runners began the longest running race ever conceived: the Trans-American Footrace. Nicknamed the Bunion Derby by newspapers, the race began at the Ascot Speedway in Los Angeles and finished 84 days later at Madison Square Garden, New York. Athletes completed a stage each day, and much like cyclists in the Tour de France, the winner was the person with the lowest accumulated time. An impressive 55 runners made it to Madison Square Garden, with Andy Payne leading the field home in 573 hours 4 minutes and 34 seconds.

Although the Trans-American Footrace eventually died out, the trail had been laid for a running challenge that continues to motivate athletes around the world. Of course, not everyone follows the route of the Bunion Derby. The lack of any organising body means that the start line can be determined by the individual. Most will, however, choose to run from West to East for the simple fact that they would be running into the sun (and often a headwind) if they went in the other direction.

Of course, with variable start and end points (not to mention a variety of possible routes along the way), the conditions and terrain during a run across America differs dramatically for one athlete to the next. Regardless, there are a number of common challenges that all have to tackle.

First and foremost there is the distance. If the runner takes the most direct route from Los Angeles to New York (avoiding major highways), they can expect to run 3,011 miles (4,846km). From San Francisco, it is 3,118 miles (5,017km). Since accurate records of these runs have been kept, 144 people have averaged between 40 and 50 miles (64-8km) per day across America, six have averaged 50-60 miles (80-96km), and just three have averaged 60-66 miles (96-106km) per day. Even if they are covering massive distances like this each day, athletes are committed to multiple months of non-stop running along predominantly cemented, often

rolling roads. While fatigue is a given in a challenge like this, running on such an unforgiving surface places enormous strain on the body. Blisters are uncomfortable but commonplace, and ankle, knee or general leg injuries are nigh on inevitable. Being able to peel through the various layers of suffering to keep on going is a must for anyone hoping to finish.

But being able to tolerate pain is just one of the psychological challenges that face athletes who run across America. They must also be able to manage their minds to process the time it takes to complete the various 'phases' of the run.

These 'phases' all offer up their own individual challenges. From The Rocky mountain passes (runners can expect anything up to 170,000ft/51,800m of elevation gain during the crossing) to vast un-populated deserts, and from rolling prairies to big city traffic, athletes crossing America will be exposed to it all. All of these differing 'worlds' bring with them contrasting climates. Athletes attempting to complete the run must, therefore, be ready to tackle sub-zero temperatures in the mountains, the intense heat of the desert, torrential rains and strong winds. Running through inclement conditions is tough when an athlete is 'fresh'; doing so when fatigued is nigh on torturous.

right The road across America crosses mountains and deserts

There is another major consideration that transcontinental runners have to take into account: other road users. Legally, pedestrians are not allowed to use Interstate roads in the USA (special exemptions have been made for certain runners). So while the athletes do not have to deal with the inevitable dangers of running on busy highways, many of the roads that they do use still carry large volumes of traffic. What's more, most of this traffic is not expecting to share the road with pedestrians. Safety is, of course, paramount in these situations, and most of the time the runner will rely on a support crew to ensure that passing traffic gives them a wide berth.

Despite the booming popularity of ultra endurance races, the record for the run across America is a longstanding one. In 1980, Frank Giannino Jr. completed his 3,100 mile (4,989km) run from San Francisco to New York in 46 days 8 hours and 36 minutes. In 2012, a new race was launched: the Run Across America On Trail. Using only canal and train trails, the 3,302 mile (5,314km) race was won by Mike Samuelson in 719 hours 47 minutes and 13 seconds (30 days).

Running across America is a formidable challenge. Years of planning coupled with months of effort sees athletes cover truly exceptional distances. In so doing they pit themselves against the best and the worst of this great country, attempting to realise the completion of one of the world's toughest running challenges.

opposite Suneson carried everything he needed in a stroller

Björn **Suneson**

The first time I didn't know anything about it and I was just focused on the running. But the more times that you do it, the more experienced you get. And it's easier every time that you do it. Now, I'm 66 years old, and my latest run was the easiest of them all because I had so much self-confidence. It's more a mental thing than a physical thing. So, this latest time, I never doubted that I would reach New York.

The reason that I've done it so many times is because of the people I meet along the road. The Americans are so nice and so very encouraging and that helps me a lot.

Of course, I have had some big difficulties in my running. The biggest challenge is when you are injured. I have been so lucky because I am almost never injured. So the biggest challenge I think is the weather. In Europe, the weather is not so bad normally. In the USA, when it is raining, it's raining ten times more than normal. When it's windy, it's much more windy. I think one of my biggest challenges was when I was almost in a tornado in South Dakota. Then you feel very, very small.

Another big challenge was when I was running in Utah, up in the mountains close to Salt Lake City. I realised that the road I was running on would end because the snow was too deep – I couldn't continue. And if I had had to turn around I would need to take a detour that would add a couple of days extra. But when you have difficulties your brain works well and you find a solution. And my solution that time was to run to the snow and then ask someone to drive me on a snowmobile over the mountain. When I look back at difficulties like that, you always find some solution.

Every morning I put my hands on my stroller at 9 a.m. and just kept on running. That was it. I just kept on running. Because I was convinced that I would reach the goal after 30-40 miles. My solution was to take it easy and be careful. When something was not going well – problems with the equipment or whatever – I tried to fix it immediately.

Normally, you should be very happy when you reach the goal. Most of the time my children are at the Atlantic. But the finish day is not very special. You are not more happy that day than the other days because you think 'now it's over'. You are not happy or sad. Afterwards, when I have finished, my solution is to continue as I have always done. After being at home a couple of weeks I start thinking about a new run.

Björn Suneson has run across America on four different occasions. For more information, visit: www.suneson.se.

Type Trekking & mountaineering
Date November – February
Distance 1,864 miles (3,000 km)
Main obstacles Conditions, Terrain, Cold

Competitors say
❝You're on the bottom of the world, on the top of an ice cap, in the middle of the universe – then you feel very lonely.❞
Børge Ousland

Trek Solo Across Antarctica

'Men wanted for hazardous journey. Low wages, bitter cold, long hours of complete darkness. Safe return doubtful.' So goes the apocryphal advert that Ernest Shackleton is said to have placed in a newspaper ahead of the Imperial Trans-Antarctic Expedition. While the wording of the message may seem whimsical, it is broadly correct; crossing Antarctica is one of the hardest, most dangerous expeditions on the planet.

below Børge Ousland crossed Antarctica in just over two months

Shackleton's plan was, on paper, quite simple: sail as far as he could into the Weddell Sea, send a second ship to the Ross Ice Shelf and walk between the two of them via the South Pole. There were, however, numerous problems with it: scurvy was still an issue for explorers in the 1900s,

Shackleton proposed to walk through a largely unchartered part of the continent, and their equipment wasn't up to scratch. In the end it didn't matter; Shackleton's ship was crushed by sea ice and he never reached Antarctica. He did, however, gain considerable fame by leading one of the greatest survival stories in the history of exploration.

Even with advancements in knowledge, equipment and nutrition, it took nearly 100 years for an expedition to finally complete Shackleton's journey. In 1997, Norwegian polar explorer Børge Ousland became the first person to complete a crossing of Antarctica, doing so solo and unassisted. Setting off from Berkner Island in the Weddell Sea, Ousland trekked up towards the South Pole and then down to McMurdo Sound (the base established by Robert Falcon Scott and the ultimate goal for Shackleton). He completed the 1,864 miles (3,000km) in just over two months. It was Ousland's second attempt at an Antarctic crossing, the first having been abandoned because of frostbite and injury at the South Pole, some 620 miles (1,000km) into the journey.

There are numerous reasons why crossing Antarctica – either solo or as part

of a team – is an extreme challenge. Fundamentally, though, Antarctica is not designed for human beings. For starters, the weather can be horrendous. The continent is plagued by violent and unpredictable storms that bring with them hurricane-force katabatic winds and large quantities of snow. These storms can last for days (the one that killed Scott and his men is estimated to have lasted for nine days), and often bring with them exceptionally cold temperatures. Of course, Antarctica only gets down to its very coldest during the winter (the Russian Antarctic research station of Vostok once recorded the coldest temperature on earth: −89.2°C/-128.6°F). Ordinarily, in a 'good' summer, the temperature at the South Pole sits at around -25°C (-13°F), with wind chill adding a little bit of extra 'bite'.

Challenging weather conditions simply serve to make a difficult trek even harder. Expeditions across the ice cap expect to encounter everything from troublesome waves of sastrugi to deep snowdrifts and miles of crevasse fields. The latter, in particular, pose a very real threat to the success – and safety – of an explorer. Successfully negotiating the crevasses that line Antarctica's glaciers requires careful navigation and the ability to determine the strength of a snow bridge (very often the only way across). Crevasses can be particularly perilous for solo travellers as there is nobody to help them should they fall – as Ousland did during his crossing. In these instances, the individual has to hope their support rope catches on something solid, and that they can pull themselves out.

Because it is so large and basically uninhabited, Antarctic crossings are unassisted expeditions. As a result, explorers drag pulks (or sledges) weighing anything up to 200kg

(440lbs) behind them. These pulks contain everything they need to survive on the ice. Because there is a limit to how much a human being can drag, supplies are kept to a minimum based on a target travel schedule. As such, should anything delay the explorer (such as injury or prolonged storms), they have little in the way of contingency food, drink and equipment to help them survive.

In as much as it is a physical challenge, trekking across Antarctica is also a supreme mental test. Despite satellite

below The journey is long, lonely and very cold

phones and other communication equipment, Antarctica is an isolated continent. Those attempting to trek across it do not expect to see anybody or anything for weeks on end. Should anything happen to them it can be difficult – if not impossible – for help to arrive before the punishing conditions take their toll. What's more, much of the trekking is done through an endlessly white terrain. This lack of discernible visual stimulus can play havoc on the weary mind, with only the strongest able to cope for months on end.

Crossing Antarctica is an almighty undertaking. It challenges some of the world's toughest explorers in one of the most extreme environments on the planet. Even today, many who attempt the crossing fail. Those who succeed do so due to their indefatigable levels of resilience and strength. By completing a crossing, they conquer the loneliest, most dangerous continent on earth.

Børge Ousland

It's an endless expanse of snow. You are walking on these huge, huge ice caps with this intense cold. If you look at the big picture and imagine seeing yourself from space, you're on the bottom of the world, on the top of an ice cap in the middle of the universe – then you feel lonely. It's quite amazing to be in this loneliness and still be able to function.

It is also beautiful, with the midnight sun circling above you. With all the shapes in the snow – with the sastrugi, and the wind that has carved out all of these shapes in front of you. I think Antarctica is more like meditation compared to the North Pole. You do reach levels inside you which you didn't think existed when you are on your own for such a long time.

I think the start was probably the hardest part of the expedition. I never get used to leaving that airplane on day one on a trip like that. You never know what is going to happen, and you have two to three months in front of you, it's heavy going and nobody has done it before. It takes a couple of weeks before you have the right harmony and are used to being there. Then you are in a good flow and you can keep on going forever. You have to penetrate this landscape and make friends with it somehow, otherwise you can't do it.

The physical challenge is on two levels. One is to function in the temperatures and the wind without freezing to death or getting frostbite. The second is the long steady haul of that heavy sled. When I started on day one, my sled was 187kg because I had food and fuel for 90 days. To pull that sucks the energy out of your body. You are walking uphill for the first two months to the South Pole –

3,000 metres uphill. You have the sastrugi and you have the head winds and it is very, very, tiring. So you need to be well trained and you need to have lots of patience and have good stamina.

Coming to the end of the expedition pulling that heavy sled for two months was extremely hard. And coming through the crevasses solo was very dangerous. When you are in a group you can always rope up so if you fall into a crevasse it doesn't really matter – you have a friend who can pull you up and you are hanging on a rope. When you are solo you don't really have that. You have to cross all these crevasses and hope they will hold. I went through a crevasse one time and was hanging on the metal bars on the sled – that was what saved me from falling to the bottom.

The greatest part of finishing was the feeling that I was tough enough to start after my first attempt. I had had two attempts – the first was in 1995. Then I reached the South Pole but I got frost bite and had some injuries so had to abort. The question was then: would I dare to go again? I did that and I made it. The feeling that I was tough enough to say 'I will take the chance of another failure' and then to have the victory – that was a great feeling. Sometimes when I look back on it now I can't understand how I managed to do it.

Børge Ousland completed the first solo, un-assisted crossing of Antarctica in 1997. It is one of numerous polar expeditions the Norwegian has completed. For more information, visit: www.ousland.no.

Type Run
Date Year-round
Distance minimum 9,000 miles
(14,484km)
Main challenges Weather, distance, time,
terrain

Competitors say
*Sometimes in one day the
landscape could change three or four
times in 40km. It was amazing.*
Janette Murray-Wakelin

Run Around Australia

Australia is a land of stark extremes. The country rolls from picture-perfect coastal cities to lush green fields and the seemingly endless expanse of the Outback. Every year, thousands set out to explore this magnificent continent. But while most choose to travel by car, train or airplane, every now and again an athlete sets out on foot.

right The distances in Australia can be mind-boggling at times

As with any challenge of this nature, there is no set start or finish point for a run around Australia. Nor is there a pre-defined route. Many runners choose to follow Highway 1, which is a collection of roads that passes through all of the country's State Capitals (and effectively circumnavigates it). If runners were able to complete the challenge on Highway 1 alone, they would cover a minimum of 9,000 miles (14,484km). However, because it is not always feasible – or preferable – to follow the Highway, their journeys can easily be in excess of 10,000 miles (16,000km), if not more. For good measure, some also choose to throw in a lap of Tasmania, adding 800 miles (1,287km) to the challenge.

Perhaps the greatest obstacle that runners face to circumnavigating Australia is the country itself. Of course, there are major urban conurbations all the way along the East Coast, and in parts of the north, south and west too. But for vast tranches of the run, particularly on the north and south coasts, there is little in the way of human habitations. While the lack of company poses no significant threat to the well-being of the runner, the lack of food and drink outlets can. It goes without saying that managing nutrition and hydration on a challenge like this is essential. But it is not always easy. For instance, any runner attempting to cross the Nullabor Plain – a 600 mile (1,000km) flat, barren expanse of arid land in South Australia – has to estimate (and carry) everything that they need to survive for the duration of the crossing.

There is a reason why certain stretches of Australia are

uninhabited; put simply, they are uninhabitable. Like large swathes of the Outback, parts of the south and east of the country rarely see any rainfall and have little in the way of available ground water supplies. The sun can be relentless, and a fierce wind often blows across the pancake flat terrain. The North of the country, meanwhile, often experiences

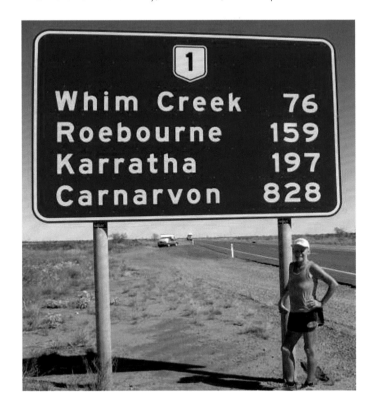

vastly different conditions. The sub-tropical Northern Territory boasts lush surrounds, but fierce heat and humidity make the living tough. Needless to say, running in either environment is beyond the physical capabilities of most athletes.

As well as the weather and the temperatures, the conditions on and around the road itself are often challenging. Of course, in populated areas the roads are well maintained and it is easy for runners to avoid oncoming traffic. However, in the more remote parts of the country this is not always the case. The highway often turns into a single-lane road, frequented by massive trucks (or road-trains) who aren't usually expecting to come across a pedestrian. More than one expedition around Australia has had to be aborted because of the danger posed by passing traffic. Of course, runners always have the option of stepping aside

when vehicles are approaching. However, in parts of the Northern Territory in particular, the surrounding verges are not only rocky and unstable, but can also be frequented by things that can give you a nasty bite. While the likelihood of being bitten is relatively small, the likelihood of tripping on rocks or twisting ankles is quite high. Any niggles or injuries sustained on a journey of this length can have a profound impact on an athlete's ability to complete their challenge.

All of these variables simply add to the magnitude of the challenge facing any runner who attempts a circumnavigation. As well as dealing with the conditions en route and the physical barriers to completion that they represent, a circumnavigation of Australia is also a psychological challenge. Any athlete attempting the run does so in the knowledge that they will spend up to a year on the road – sometimes more. They know that conditions are far from ideal, and that they will often be alone in an inhospitable environment. That is perhaps why so few people have completed this epic run.

Ron Grant was the first to finish a circumnavigation of the continent. In 1983, he ran from Brisbane to Brisbane – a total distance of 8,316 miles (13,383km) – in 217 days. Just four other people have followed in his footsteps. Deborah De Williams completed a walk/run in 2005. Janette Murray-Wakelin and Alan Murray walked and ran a marathon every day for 365 days from Melbourne to Melbourne in 2013. They added an additional marathon back to their hometown to take the world record for the most consecutive marathons (366).

What's more, they did the whole thing on a raw vegan diet.

Running around Australia is an extreme physical and mental challenge. It pits an athlete against every environment that this incredible country has to offer. It also forces them to confront the challenges posed by the sheer distance before them. It is a supreme test of endurance, and one that only a handful of people have ever been able to master.

Janette Murray-Wakelin

We trained for a couple of years beforehand, going out and running every day and putting in the miles. From that point of view, once we got started running the consecutive marathons, it took about a week for the body to settle into the fact that it was going to happen every day. After that it was fine. We were pretty physically trained by that time to keep going. It was more of a mental challenge to keep going for the full year.

We didn't sustain any injuries from running. We put that down to the diet we have and the training we did. We kept the running time at an average of six hours per day – we weren't trying to break any speed records. We did sustain injuries from falling, both of us. That was due to tripping on things at the side of the road and having to get off the road when vehicles were coming. The conditions around Australia vary depending on the area, but there were some pretty 'interesting' roads with not much of a verge to get off on and when there was there were very large stones. So it was easy to trip and fall. We got injuries from falling, but nothing that stopped us from running.

It's completely remote. There are places out there where there are no shops. You can't buy food. When we went out across the top of the Northern Territory we had to stock up. There were a few shops, but nothing that sold what we would eat or that would sustain us to run a marathon a day. Coming across the Nullabor Plain there is absolutely nothing. Not even trees. So we had to really stock up on the food and really try and get it right for the amount of days we were out there. We were only covering about 42km per day, which meant getting across these areas that were remote took a lot longer than if you were driving. For us, it was quite an accomplishment to plan it right to have enough food.

The remoteness, insofar as the mental challenge, was interesting. Especially coming across the Southern end because we had only a quarter of the way to go. Being there and seeing it was phenomenal. I wouldn't recommend people run a marathon a day to get around Australia, but I would certainly recommend that they do some of it on foot. It's the most amazing country. Every area we went to was totally different to the next. Sometimes in one day the landscape could change three or four times in 40km. It was amazing. For us, personally, it really made the difference for getting out there because you didn't know what you would come across.

We started in Melbourne and went all the way around and finished in Melbourne on day 365 – that was the end of the year. We decided on the way around to do an extra day and get the world record for consecutive marathons. Doing that extra marathon was incredible – it was a really emotional journey.

Janette Murray-Wakeling and Alan Murray completed their circumnavigation of Australia in 2013. For more information, visit: www.runningrawaroundaustralia.com.

Type Run
Date July
Distance 584 miles (939km)
Main challenges Heat, distance, elevation change

Competitors say
❝I wasn't looking for easy. I was looking for hard, challenging and extreme.❞
Lisa Smith-Batchen

Complete the Badwater Quad

From the lowest to the highest point on the contiguous United States of America by way of the hottest place on earth, the Badwater Ultramarathon is a race of extremes. But for some, this test of physical and mental strength is not enough. Instead, they choose to go back the way they came. And then they do the whole thing again.

below The road through Death Valley is long, lonely and barren

In 1977, Al Arnold was hoping to make it third time lucky. The American had twice been forced to abandon his attempt to run from Badwater, the lowest place in the western hemisphere, to Mount Whitney, the highest place in the contiguous United States of America. After setting up a treadmill in a sauna and training religiously for this latest attempt, Arnold believed that he was ready. He was right.

The run to Mount Whitney took him 84 hours and he lost 8% of his total body weight. That didn't matter, because Arnold had proved that it could be done. Just a few years later, the Badwater Ultramarathon became a near-permanent fixture on the ultramarathon calendar.

Death Valley, the setting for the start of the Badwater Ultramarathon, is a brutal place. The surrounding mountains trap heat from the near-incessant sun, leading to extremes of temperature (in 1913, Death Valley recorded the hottest ever temperature on earth: 56.7°C/134°F). Badwater – the eponymous start line of the race – lies at the heart of Death Valley on the shores of a vast salt lake. The air is dry, the heat is relentless and shade comes at a premium.

As soon as an athlete attempting the Ultramarathon and starts their run, they are given a brutal introduction to what lies ahead. Following the road through the lunar landscape around Badwater, runners pass the oasis of Furnace Creek and then head out on the lonely road towards Stovepipe Wells. Salt flats suck the moisture out of the air, sand dunes creep up towards the slopes of distant mountains, and the hot desert winds are relentless. Temperatures are fierce. The thermometer can easily push 49°C (120°F) during a July day (with ground temperature even more), and there have been nights when the mercury hovers around 37°C (100°F).

Beyond Stovepipe Wells, the climbing begins. Fifty miles (80km) in, runners climb up towards Towne Pass (1510m/4956ft). A 17 mile tight, mountain road, this is the first time that conditions start to change and the

temperature drops – it will not be the last. The 10 mile descent on the other side places pressure on fatigued limbs, and is followed by another steep climb and a second tough descent. With 90 miles (145km) of the run complete, the impact of the course and the conditions really start to take their toll on competitors.

After another (steep) climb, competitors are likely to get their first glimpse of Mount Whitney. A long, undulating and severely testing road takes them towards the town of Lone Pine, which presents the gateway to Whitney Portal. The climate here differs wildly from that in Death Valley, and runners (and their support crews) have to be prepared for strong winds, hailstorms and frigid temperatures. The official race finish line is at 2,548m (8,360ft) – the Mount Whitney trailhead. In fact, once they reach the Mount Whitney trailhead they have

something to eat, maybe rest a little, and then run back the way that they came.

But there are those that aspire to do more.

The Badwater Double (essentially there and back) is an increasingly popular challenge. However, some have also attempted the Badwater Triple, and just two people – Marshall Ulrich and Lisa Smith-Batchen – have completed the Badwater Quad (a double double). In so doing, they covered 584 miles (939km) and experienced upwards of 96,000ft (29,260m) in elevation change. Completing Badwater once is an impressive physical and mental achievement. Doing so four times back-to-back is remarkable.

To be successful runners have to adapt and perform in both extremes of heat (in Death Valley) and cold (Mount Whitney). What's more, they have to be ready to run for days on end. Managing the body through these conditions is far from easy, with nutrition and hydration especially

above Temperatures in Death Valley can easily hit 49C / 120F

left Lisa Smith Batchen completed the Badwater Quad in 2014

important when it comes to desert racing. Like many extreme challenges, even seemingly insignificant mistakes can have a profound impact on the outcome.

Marshall Ulrich was the first to complete the Quad in 2001 in 10 days. Lisa Smith-Batchen followed in his footsteps and completed it in 2014 in 15 days.

In 2014, the Death Valley Park Service decided to ban the Badwater Ultramarathon pending an investigation This ban was only temporary and the original race is once again on the endurance calendar. Regardless of a ban, any Double, Triple or Quad attempt at Badwater falls outside the remit of the Ultramarathon race organisers. It is an entirely independent challenge, and as such all logistics and planning are the responsibility of the runner and their team.

Completing Badwater is impressive. Doing it twice is exceptional. Doing it four times is an extreme take on one of the world's toughest challenges. Only the strongest athletes attempt this challenge, and even then not all are successful. Completing the Badwater Quad is a truly remarkable physical achievement in this land of extremes.

Lisa Smith-Batchen

The day that I started the air temperature was 127 °F, so the ground temperature was even hotter. We were thrown sandstorms and head winds and thunder and lightning in the desert. It's just a harsh environment – it's almost indescribable unless you're out there and can feel the heat. It's wild. There's no shade, and nowhere to run and hide. The sun is incredibly intense out there – so intense that you can die. In fact, when I did my run someone went out for a four mile walk at Furnace Creek and died after two miles – that was two days before I finished my run. That's how intense it is. You cannot take that harshness for granted, it will zap the life out of you.

The hardest part for me was on the second leg. I got the first one done and felt great, summited Mount Whitney and felt really great. Then for 24 hours I had massive stomach problems, diarrhoea, couldn't keep anything down, lacked energy. I felt awful. Every mile I stopped off the side of the road. Everything I ate shot through me. It was so miserable for that 24 hours that I never want to go through it again. But I never thought that I wouldn't make it, it was just 'how do I get through this?'

At the start of the last leg I felt great. I felt really, really fit. I came down Mount Whitney and everyone told me to take a nap. I hadn't slept for 38 hours but I was full of energy. I ran down the portal road, and ran into Lone Pine – I was doing 8 minute miles. I got faster on the fourth leg. I was running 7 minute miles going into the end of it. You feel so alive – it was like the horse going back to the stable. Once the third leg was done, I knew I would make it. That third lap was really tough, and then on the fourth everything clicks and you feel like you have it.

The reason I did it in July was because it was the hottest conditions and it was the hardest place to go and do it. I wasn't looking for easy. I was definitely looking for hard, challenging and extreme. I got exactly what I wanted. I had no aches and pains. I walked away with three blisters. Of course, I had extreme fatigue, sleep deprivation and had lost 18lbs, but I was left with immense gratitude.

Lisa Smith-Batchen completed the Badwater Quad in 2014 to raise money for cleaner water. For more information, visit: www.badwater4goodwater.com.

Type Walk
Date Year-round
Distance 4,345 miles (6,992km)
Main obstacles Terrain, hygiene, wildlife

Competitors say
❝ *If you were to say "would you want to walk the Amazon today?", I would say "no", because the dangers are too high.* ❞
Ed Stafford

Walk the Length of the Amazon

Since Francisco de Orellana became the first person to navigate the length of the Amazon, few have dared to follow in his footsteps. There is a reason for that. The Amazon River is not only an enormous body of water, but a dangerous one, too. It challenges explorers on every level, bringing them into contact with deadly animals, nigh on impenetrable rainforest, and sweltering heat. It is a river – and land – of massive extremes.

above It took Ed Stafford more than two years to walk the length of the Amazon

Since Orellana completed his legendary journey along the Amazon, just five expeditions have successfully travelled from the source of the river to its mouth. Just one has done so on foot. In 2010, Ed Stafford became the first person to walk the entire 4,345 miles (6,992km) from the Nevado Mismi glacier in the Peruvian Andes to the Atlantic Ocean. For good measure, Stafford began his expedition from the Peruvian town of Camana, and in so doing walked from the West to the East coast of South America.

Regardless of the means of travel, any expedition along the length of the Amazon is fraught with difficulties. Of them all, perhaps the greatest threat to success comes from some of the people who reside along the river. Parts of the Amazon skirt through lawless regions of Peru and Colombia, where drug trafficking is rife and outsiders are not welcome. Local tribes, too, are often suspicious of 'foreigners', and are ready to attack with arrows and spears if they feel threatened. Of course, this is the minority. During Stafford's journey most people he met were welcoming, and simply wanted to know why he was making such a crazy journey.

It is a good question.

The Amazon rainforest is a difficult place to explore. Jungle trekking is notoriously hard work, with expeditions like Stafford's repeatedly forced to break virgin paths through mile after mile of thick rainforest vines, brambles and thorns. This trekking is further complicated during the rainy season, when the flat area around the Amazon Basin gets flooded. When the basin becomes inundated, expeditions are forced to wade through inky-black water that can easily be chest-deep, if not deeper. Needless to say that, despite the water levels, vines and thorns remain an ever-present fixture, and so the expedition must carry on hacking a path through the now submerged forest. It is not only slow, but incredibly uncomfortable work.

This style of trekking also brings with it obvious health risks. Cleanliness is far from easy in the jungle, but is essential when it comes to maintaining forward momentum. Feet have to be cleaned every day, water and food constantly

checked and inevitable stomach ailments dealt with. What's more, cuts, bites and sores are all part and parcel of the Amazon experience, and in the jungle environment they can very easily become infected.

Then there are the animals. Amazon is famous for its piranhas, jaguars, anacondas and crocodiles. However, it is the smaller 'pests' that are more likely to jeopardise the success of a jungle expedition. Malarial mosquitos, parasitic botflies and biting sand flies are just some of the critters that regularly plague expeditions at all stages of the journey. Their repeated bites are not only uncomfortable, but can damage morale after days of unforgiving jungle trekking.

Of course, on top of all of these obstacles is the simple fact that trekking the length of the Amazon is an enormous physical and mental challenge. The latter in particular is crucial, with adventurers having to stay calm in the face of danger, to keep moving when physically exhausted, and to be able to ignore the inevitable pain and discomfort that comes from trekking through the world's largest rainforest. That is, perhaps, why so few people have ever managed to complete this expedition.

After Francesco de Orellana, John Ridgway completed the first documented expedition from the source to mouth of the Amazon in 1970. When Ed Stafford completed his journey in 2010, it was only the fifth time that an expedition had successfully completed the challenge – and the first time it was done entirely on foot. It took Stafford 2 years, 4 months and 8 days (860 days in total) to complete a trek that was – with the addition of the walk from the Peruvian coast – 4,490 miles (7,225km) in total. From start to finish, it was a brutal expedition through an extreme environment that few humans dare to tackle.

Ed Stafford

I remember saying to people 'I quite fancy walking the length of the Amazon' and it really annoyed me because everybody said, 'You can't do that, it's impossible'. That was like a red rag to a bull. I suppose the idea was born out of a contrariness or stubbornness because I really believed that it was physically possible. And when I realised that it was a world first I thought it was amazing.

I walked for two years with a Peruvian guide called Cho and we would often do little risk assessments and the risk would come out as totally unacceptable, and then we would grin at each other and say, 'We've come this far, let's just get on with it'. We knew it would be a bit dangerous, but I just trusted my experience and my skills to get us out of problems.

There were situations where I was lucky. We were held at arrow point by indigenous Indians a couple of times, given death threats quite regularly, held at gunpoint by drugs traffickers, and I was arrested for murder at one point because a man in the village went missing. I always came back to the fact that I'm not a threat to these people. I deliberately walked without a weapon and everyone I spoke to said I was crazy. But I always maintained that I was a big enough threat to the villagers as a 6' 1" white man without being armed. I took faith in human kindness.

My view of the jungle was slightly skewed because I have done a lot of expeditions and I call myself jungle-wise. For the vast majority of it there are no paths. And we walked through two Amazonian flood seasons. All of the Amazon basin is flat so as soon as the water rises it goes into the rainforest and causes this bizarre environment called flooded forest. It could be waist height, chest height or, at times, above head height. At that point we would either have to back track, or inflate the little pack raft that we had and literally it would be me at the front of the raft trying to cut through the jungle. When we could walk through the flooded forest, the way wasn't clear and the water was often jet black. So you're cutting through these brambles and thorns underwater – it was bizarre walking conditions. Horrendous.

People often ask about why my feet didn't fall apart in those conditions and I guess the answer is that it gets dark at 6 p.m. at the equator and doesn't get light until 6 a.m. We decided that we wouldn't walk at night, so we would make camp just before it got dark and wash in the river and clean our clothes and socks and hang them over the fire to dry. We'd powder our feet with medicated powder. I think that 12 hours of the feet being completely dry, powdered and clean was enough for it to be sustainable.

The big threats weren't a concern – the jaguars and things like that. Everyone thought we were crazy walking through the jungle without a shotgun. But I always maintained jaguars weren't a realistic threat as we were making loads of noise, smashing through the jungle and we weren't the size of prey they go for. The things that did get me down and that chipped away at morale was the mosquitos. The ants in certain places were horrendous – you would put your hand on a tree and 50 ants have bitten you on your arm before you've even noticed. And the sand flies – I got leishmaniasis from the sand flies which is a skin wasting disease. It's not serious in itself but it took about three months before I could get it checked out. But overall we were lucky – we didn't get malaria, typhoid or dengue fever or anything like that.

I still wonder whether finishing was the best day of my life. I think it was. There was so much relief. There had been so much worry over the last nine months – we were illegal in Brazil because we had run out of park permits so were hiding from the police. I was so emotional.

Ed Stafford was the first human being to walk the length of the Amazon. There are DVDs and books available about his expedition. For more information, visit: www.edstafford.org.

AROUND
THE
WORLD

Type Trekking & Mountaineering
Date Year-round
Distance Varies
Main challenges Cold, terrain, logistics, altitude

Competitors say
There was so much open water, we would have to swim these leads and there were huge polar bear tracks – everything was so hard.
Ryan Waters

Complete the Explorers' Grand Slam

To stand on either Pole or the highest point on earth is a significant achievement in its own right. However, for a small group of explorers these places are stepping stones towards an even more remarkable accomplishment: completing the Explorers' Grand Slam.

Completing The Explorers' Grand Slam involves trekking to the geographic North and South Poles, and climbing the highest mountains on each of the seven continents. These are: Mount Everest (Asia), Mount Kilimanjaro (Africa), Denali (North America), Aconcagua (South America), Mount Elbrus (Europe), Vinson Massif (Antarctica) and Carstensz Pyramid (New Guinea). Because the Slam is an arbitrary challenge, there are a few variations on it. Some choose to trek from the 'last degree of latitude' to both poles, a journey of approximately 60 nautical miles (111km). However, those attempting a 'true' Grand Slam begin their polar treks from a coastal point, and so complete a much longer, harder journey.

The skill set required to climb any one of the seven summits is entirely different to those needed to successfully complete a polar trek. The means of travel, the speed and demands of the expedition, and an understanding of the terrain all vary dramatically. What's more, it is not advisable to attempt to learn these skills 'on the job'. The mountains can be dangerous, while the remote and inaccessible poles are often deadly.

It is the remoteness of the South Pole that makes trekking there such a tremendous physical and mental challenge. Not only is the journey long, but the conditions en route are extreme. Crevasses are a near-permanent threat on a polar plateau that can be covered in anything from waist-deep snow to hard-packed sastrugi (ice ridges). Weather conditions on this plateau are unpredictable, with summer temperatures usually hovering around -25°C (-13°F) with added wind chill. Few people have been able to complete a trek from the coast to the pole, and a number have died trying.

At the other end of the world the conditions are even worse. Although the North Pole is relatively 'flat', the ice is anything but. Massive pressure ridges are just as likely to block the path to the pole as an open lead is. What's more, the polar ice sheet is almost constantly shifting south. As such, while expeditions are figuring out how to negotiate pressure ridges or cross leads with their pulks, they are being carried away from their goal. This ice movement is nigh-on permanent, but occasionally changes in speed and direction. As such, anyone attempting to reach the North Pole has to constantly re-negotiate their path across the ice.

Things are only a little easier in the mountains. Every big mountain needs to be treated with respect. The biggest of them all, Mount Everest (8,848m/29,035ft), perhaps warrants more than the others. Yes, Everest is now the most commercially lucrative climbing site in the world. That does not mean, however, that it is an easy mountain to summit. The sheer scale of it poses a significant physical challenge to every climber – regardless of their ability. The weather can be unpredictable, with fierce storms leaving unstable sections of snow and ice. As such, the risk of ice fall or avalanche is severe.

Of the remaining summits, two others stand out in terms of their raw physical difficulties: Denali (6,168m/20,237ft) and Carstenz Pyramid (4,884m/16,024ft). Denali is not just a tough technical climb, but as the most northerly of the seven summits it also attracts a rare breed of inclement weather. Carstenz Pyramid, meanwhile, is unique among these

mountains. Climbing high out of the New Guinea jungle, its bare, rocky slopes are near-vertical at times. As such, it is the only one of the peaks that demands technical rock climbing skills.

Only 13 people have managed to complete the 'True' Explorers' Grand Slam (another 27 have completed the Last Degree Grand Slam). British adventurer David Hempleman-Adams was the first to do so in 1998, while Norwegian Cecilie Skog was the first woman to do so. The late, great South Korean climber Park Young-Seok upped the stakes of the Grand Slam by climbing all of the 8,000 metre mountains in the world, plus trekking to the North and South Poles. He is the only person to have managed the feat.

The Explorers' Grand Slam is a true test of the world's best adventurers. It not only challenges their mental and physical strength, but their ability to adapt to different environments and challenges too. It does so on some of the most extreme terrain on the planet, where mishaps or mistakes can be severely punished. Perhaps that is the attraction of the Grand Slam – and the reason that so few people have been able to complete it.

opposite Only 13 people have completed the 'True' Explorers Grand Slam

Ryan Waters

It was a long process for me because it was something that I never really set out to do. I was interested in climbing mountains 13 years ago – I was already a rock climber. I knew about the seven summit thing, but I never set out to climb the seven summits. I was guiding people and ended up climbing them anyway. Then, in 2009 and 2010, an expedition partner of mine and I skied across Antarctica; it was the first unassisted and unsupported crossing. So then I had skied to the South Pole and after that I thought I might as well do the North Pole too, because that would top it off.

It requires surprisingly different skill sets. I had been a mountaineer for a long time and felt very comfortable in extreme environments and on expeditions. And then going into this polar ski world, I thought that it would be pretty easy to transition. And a lot of the skills do translate from high altitude mountaineering. But there are so many specific skills that are just related to polar ski expeditions that it was a pretty steep learning curve.

Climbing high altitude peaks is often a slower up and down process. You come back to a comfortable place, like a Base Camp. You have downtime and can totally relax. Whereas the polar ski expeditions are all about efficiency and constantly moving. Every system has to be very dialled and you don't take any extra stuff. It's all about getting from Point A to Point B in the most efficient manner.

In terms of challenges, the North Pole is in a league of its own. Doing a full unsupported trip is the hardest thing by far that I have ever done. There's so much local knowledge to be able to do that trip – the problem solving and getting past these open water leads. There are all these little tricks.

There were a few challenging moments. Ironically, the last four days to reach the North Pole were the hardest. We were still pretty far away – we had 120 nautical miles to cover and only a couple of weeks to get there. We basically skied for two weeks with almost no sleep. And when we got close to the Pole – for the last four days – we didn't have days and nights anymore because of the 24 hour sunlight. We skied the whole time. We would put up our tent for a three hour break and then start again. There was so much drift on the ice that we couldn't afford to sleep a full night because we would drift four miles backwards. So we essentially stopped doing that and just skied all the time. We were falling asleep on our skis. There was so much open water, we would have to swim these leads and there were huge polar bear tracks – everything was so hard and really emotional.

In the mountains, many things stand out: accidents with other teams I was involved in; helping people who have been in avalanches; having close calls myself; hard days in Pakistan. But the North Pole stands out. We didn't even know if we would get there in the last hour. There was a strong head wind and the drift was so fast that when we looked at our GPS we could see it moving us south.

Ryan Waters is a mountain guide and was the first American to complete the Explorers' Grand Slam. For more information, visit: www.ryanwaters.net.

Type Sailing
Date Year-round
Distance minimum 21,600 nautical miles
(40,003km)
Main challenges Conditions, weather

Competitors say
❝If you drive down the motorway, in the rain, with the roof down in pitch black without headlights – that's what I was sailing in.❞
Dee Caffari

Westerly Solo Sail Around the World

A solo circumnavigation of the globe is the ultimate sailing challenge. It pits the world's best mariners against cyclonic storms and massive waves on the mighty Southern Ocean. Most sailors choose an easterly route, sailing with the prevailing winds and currents. A select few, however, turn 'right' at the bottom of the world. In so doing, they sail into the eye of the storm…

below Sailing Westerly means sailing in to the wind and currents

For many of the world's best sailors, the pinnacle of their sport is a single-handed, non-stop solo circumnavigation of the planet. Although there is no set route for this journey, in races like the Vendée Globe sailors head south from Europe and cross the equator before passing Cape Horn, the Cape of Good Hope and Cape Leeuwin as part of a 24,480 mile (39,396km) expedition. For any attempt to be recognised as a circumnavigation, the sailor must have covered at least 21,600 nautical miles (40,003km), not crossed land and not sailed below the latitude of 63°S.

Despite the formidable challenges that a conventional round-the-world attempt poses, there is a small group of sailors – six, to be precise – who have chosen to take this already difficult challenge to the extremes. Whereas most sailors cross the equator and head east as they hit the Southern Ocean, these sailors have chosen to go in a westerly direction. By doing this, they sail directly into the ocean's prevailing headwinds and currents. In effect, they are sailing the 'wrong' way around the world.

Skilled mariners are more than adept at sailing their boats against the winds and currents – it is a relatively common happenstance. Using a technique known as tacking, they can force a boat upstream or against the wind to reach their desired destination. If they stop at any point, the wind or the current pushes them backwards. On normal waters this presents few significant challenges.

But the Southern Ocean is not a normal body of water. To start with, it is enormous. As such, sailors attempting to go the 'wrong' way face months of tacking (and all that this entails) in a challenging environment. This adds considerable distance to the journey, with sailors having to point their boats away from their goal to counter the contrary conditions.

This also means that they are constantly sailing into the areas of low pressure that develop in the Southern Ocean. The conditions in the south are notoriously severe, in part because of the lack of land to arrest the development of weather systems and cyclonic storms. These storms can be ferocious, bringing with them swells up to 6oft (18m) high, gale-force winds and large volumes of rain, hail and snow. Maintaining forward momentum against these conditions is not only difficult, but can be downright dangerous as the boat is tossed between walls of icy water.

Of course, the monohulls used in these single-handed attempts are designed to perform in these conditions. However, having the confidence to let them do so is another matter altogether. Sailors – regardless of their direction of travel – repeatedly refer to being on the edge of control in the Southern Ocean. If they lose that control, or the boat gets damaged during a storm, it is up to them alone to rectify the situation. Sailors on round-the-world attempts have been forced to fix damage to the hull of their boat, or scale 6oft (18m) masts in the middle of a cyclone – both incredibly dangerous things to do. If the boat is irreparably damaged, they may be forced to spend days in icy water, clinging to their capsized craft while they await rescue.

Because of the severity of the challenge, sailing the wrong way around the world is a physically and mentally exhausting experience. Constantly tacking against the ocean is an gruelling process. Sleep comes at a premium during the journey, and is usually taken in short spells (which can amount to as little as four hours per day). Meanwhile, conditions on board the boats are cramped, with kit constantly wet because of the short gaps between low pressure systems.

This confluence of challenges means that only a handful of people have managed to successfully complete a single-handed westerly circumnavigation of the globe. Sir Chay Blythe was the first to do so in 1971. In 2004, Jean Luc

Van Den Heede broke the record for the fastest westerly circumnavigation, completing his journey in 122 days 14 hours 3 minutes and 49 seconds. Two years later Dee Caffari became the first woman to complete the challenge, finishing in 178 days.

The fact that only six people (at the time of writing) have been able to complete a westerly circumnavigation of the world is indicative of the challenge that it presents to sailors. Nothing about this expedition is easy – or comfortable. What's more, everything is loaded against the sailor, and if anything goes wrong, it tends to do so spectacularly. It is an extreme challenge on every level, and one that only a select group are able to complete.

above It is a challenging, lonely journey around the world

Jean Luc Van Den Heede

I have sailed four times around the world – twice in the BOC and twice in the Vendée Globe. The last time I was doing it, I thought about going the wrong way. So after two years of thinking about what could happen, I decided to do it.

There are a lot of differences when you sail the wrong way. When you are in the Vendée Globe – or you race the 'right' way – you are pushed by the winds and pushed by the waves. The boat is going very fast and you are surfing on the waves. You are going 15-20 knots, sometimes more. It's fun to put the boat like a surfboard on the wave. All of the new generation of sailors like it – the speed, the stress of the boat going very fast down the waves.

When you go the other way, first the boat goes very slowly. You cannot go direct because you are 55 degrees to the wind so you have to tack several times. You are going maximum 10 or 11 knots when the sea is flat. It is not so much fun – it is why there are only six people who have done it. The other problem is that you are not going with the low pressure – you are going against it. When you are going against the wind, the low pressure stays for one or two days maximum, so the wind changes a lot more and you have to change the sails a lot more. All of this makes it a lot harder – it is what attracted me.

The most difficult thing is to accept that the boat is not going in the right direction. You want to go west but you cannot go west. You are at 30 or 40 degrees to the west. So at the end of the day, if you sail 200 miles only 100 are in the right direction. That is frustrating. Also, the waves are against you and against the boat.

The other thing that is difficult is that everything is wet. It is very hard to find something that is dry. In the Vendée Globe, sometimes you have a nice day. You have one or two days when you can dry your clothes, have a bit of sun and take care of yourself. When you are going the other way, sometimes you have five or six hours of dry weather, but the low pressure is always coming and so you have very little time to change and prepare for it.

To finish ... you cannot describe what you think. The challenge is very hard and so you are very happy. You are so happy to arrive at your goal.

Most of the time, you do things because you take pleasure in them. For this, you cannot believe that pleasure is important. You have to be prepared mentally to do it, and you have to forget all of

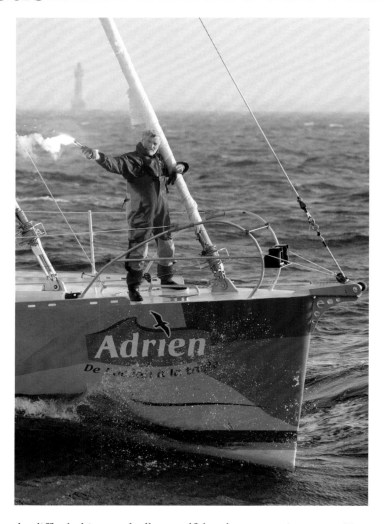

the difficult things and tell yourself that they are not important. To be wet is not so important, to be thirsty is not important, to force yourself to wake up when you are warm and dry ... not important. If comfort is important to you, it's not a good thing to do.

Jean Luc Van Den Heede holds the westerly record for a circumnavigation of the globe (122d 14h 3m 49s). For more information, visit: www.vdh.fr.

Type Walk/Run
Date Year-round
Distance circa 22,858 miles (36,787.559km)
Main challenges Terrain, psychology, climate

Competitors say
❝The reason it took so long is because it was very, very hard.❞
Rosie Swale-Pope

A Pedestrian Circumnavigation of the World

Every year thousands of people set off to travel around the world. Most go as part of a once-in-a-lifetime adventure, travelling by planes, trains and automobiles. But there are a select few, who like to take their time. Who strap a rucksack to their back or load up a buggy and set out on an epic adventure. Their adventure begins with a single step, and will end many years later. These are the people who travel the world on foot. Some of them walk it, one or two have even attempted to run it. All who finish their challenge can lay claim to a circumnavigation of unparalleled endurance.

right Any circumnavigation of the globe is not just a massive physical undertaking, it's a challenging logistical exercise too

Because of the nature of walking the world, there are no official 'rules' about what that actually entails. According to the World Runners Association an attempt should start and finish in the same place, cover at least 16,155 miles (26,000km) and cross four continents. The Guinness Book of Records has different stipulations for recognition, underlining the arbitrary nature of these rules.

American David Kunst is widely recognised as being the first person to make a verified circumnavigation of the globe as per the Guinness Book of Records rules. He completed 14,450 miles (23,250km) walk in just over four years (June 1970 to October 1974).

However, Kunst was certainly not the first to complete the challenge. Very little is known of American George Matthew Schilling, who reputedly became the first person to walk around the world between 1897 and 1904. A lot more, however, is known about Romanian Dumitru Dan, who not only completed the journey but produced plenty of corroborative evidence with it. After reading about a challenge to walk the world set by the Touring Club de France in 1910, Dan set off with three friends to see if they could claim the 100,000 franc prize. Starting off from Romania, Dan walked more than 62,137 miles (100,000km) during his attempt. His three friends (and dog) all died, and he had

to pause for a few years to return to Europe for World War One with just 2,485 miles (4000km) left to walk. Dan finally completed the journey more than 13 years after it began. He had worn through 497 pairs of peasant shoes and, because of the Great War, the value of his 100,000 franc

opposite
The current record for running around the world is an impressive 621 days

reward had diminished significantly.

Unsurprisingly, only a handful of individuals have followed in the footsteps of these pioneering walkers, and not all of them have abided by Guinness Book of Records 'rules'. Christian preacher Arthur Blessitt began walking in 1969 and has since covered 40,600 miles (65,339km). At the time of writing he was still walking. Meanwhile, Ffyona Campbell was the first woman to walk around the world, finishing her epic (and somewhat controversial) journey in 1994.

There are plenty of reasons why so few people have completed a pedestrian circumnavigation of the globe. First and foremost, there are the time and logistical considerations attached to such a challenge. World-walkers can expect to spend many years alone on the road. Loneliness is an inevitable consequence of this, with walkers and runners often struggling to maintain their motivation. Feelings of isolation can be exacerbated by the logistical

difficulties that often blight an attempt. Visa complications are commonplace (one round-the-world attempt was delayed for five years while the walker received clearance to enter Russia). So, too, are route changes. Many attempts pass through geo-politically sensitive regions, and so last minute diversions are almost inevitable.

Such difficulties can be particularly challenging in the face of both extreme cumulative fatigue and bouts of inclement weather. While the former is nigh on mandatory for any endurance athlete attempting to overcome a formidable challenge such as this, the latter is a certainty. Even the fastest runners will spend up to two years on their journey, and so can expect to encounter both the best - and the worst - of what the world has to offer.

As is the nature of challenges such as this, some walk while others choose to run. In 2003, Briton Robert Garside arrived at India Gate in New Delhi, becoming the first person

below Walking or running around the world can be a long, lonely journey

to run around the world in line with Guinness rules. During his 35,000 mile (56,327km) journey, Garside ran through 29 countries on six continents over a period of 2,062 days. Briton Kevin Carr, meanwhile, set the World Runners Association record for the fastest circumnavigation in 2015. Carr covered 16,300 miles (26,232km) in 621 days. Not everyone abides by the rules, though. British adventurer Rosie Swale-Pope completed a Northern Hemisphere circumnavigation in 2008, covering 19,900 miles (32,000km) in just under five years.

A journey of a thousand miles starts with a single step. The same is true for a journey of 16,000 miles. One single step has launched a small group of individuals on a journey of unprecedented duration, laden with physical and psychological challenges, and sometimes fraught with danger. To complete the challenge requires unprecedented levels of resolve and fortitude. Not to mention a good pair of shoes (or two).

Rosie **Swale-Pope**

I have always struggled with running – I started when I was nearly 50. I did the Marathon des Sables where I learnt to run with a rucksack. Then every year I would go on a little run (1000 miles across Iceland – that kind of thing) and write a few articles. Every year I learnt how to live in a ditch and carry minimal stuff. When my husband died of cancer I ran some marathons and then looked at a map of the world and decided to run around it – I'm a believer that inside darkness there is light.

I was very, very upset and heartbroken and didn't want to be saying 'please help me' for fundraising, so I used my savings and had some terrific equipment (which is the basis of success) and just went for it. It was an exciting, difficult and gorgeous journey.

My idea was to run a circle around the world, not to run across every continent with expensive airfares. I ran from my home to Harwich, took the ferry to Holland and then ran to Moscow and on through Siberia. I took a plane across the Bering Sea as there was no ice. It was wonderful to run under the Northern Lights and to be alone. It's not easy when you're out there in a tent because you've got to face things – like when a wolf put its head in my tent or I had frostbite.

I chose the tough route because it was the cheapest, but also because this vast swathe of land fascinated me. I had two winters in Russia. I was nearly swept away by rivers in the summer, nearly froze to death in the winter – it reached -62°C. The reason it took so long is because it was very, very hard. In the summer – when I was trying to escape the winter – I sometimes did 27 miles per day, but more usually 15 miles. But in the winter I would maybe do 5 miles per day, and there were some days when I would do 100 yards per day – dragging myself and equipment across the snow. It was very, very tough.

It was the closest thing between beauty and hardship that I have ever experienced. The people I met made the difference to me. The physical journey was relatively easy compared to the mental journey.

Rosie Swale-Pope is an author, adventurer and marathon runner who successfully completed a five-year around-the-world run. For more information, visit: www.rosieswalepope.co.uk.

Type Cycle
Date Year-round
Distance 24,900 miles (40,073km)
Main obstacles Fatigue, loneliness, conditions

Competitors say
You realise you have to hit the lows to get the highs. You can endure anything after that.
Juliana Buhring

Cycle Around the World

Cycling around the world is, quite simply, the ultimate bike ride. There is no pre-determined course. There are no time limits. But there are a couple of 'rules' (if a cyclist is aiming at a spot in the Guinness Book of Records, anyway).

right Because of the nature of the challenge, there is no pre-defined route around the world...

To be recognised by 'the Book', a rider must finish where they started. In so doing they must have travelled at least the length of the equator (24,900 miles/40,073km), of which 18,000 miles (28,968km) must have been ridden. They can travel east to west or west to east and they have to cross two antipodal points. That's it. Cyclists are allowed to use other forms of transport to cross things like water, but for the most part everything has to be done on two wheels.

Of course, for the majority who tackle this challenge, a ride around the world is a fantastic adventure. It is an experience to be savoured at a leisurely pace. It is, quite simply, an opportunity to wander the world in a unique way. But not everybody approaches the challenge with this mindset. In fact, a small group of cyclists view a ride around the world as an opportunity to test their physical and mental strength. In the process, they are looking to claim a spot in the Guinness Book of Records.

Currently, Great Britain's Alan Bate is recognised as holding the fastest time for a circumnavigation of the globe on two wheels. Bate completed his journey in 106 days 10hrs and 33mins in 2010. Briton Mike Hall managed the circumnavigation in just 91 days and 18 hours in 2012, but changes to the rules laid out by the Guinness Book of Records (to include transit time) means that Bate's time remains the one to beat. In 2012, Juliana Buhring became the fastest woman to complete the circumnavigation under Guinness World Record rules in a time of 152 days.

The challenges faced by those attempting to cycle around the world – particularly those doing it against the clock – are

opposite
Juliana Buhring circumnavigated the globe in 152 days – a World Record

considerable. First and foremost, cycling around the world is a huge physical undertaking. To complete the 18,000 mile (28,968km) ride in a little over 91 days, Mike Hall had to average nearly 200 miles (321km) per day. For an experienced rider, logging 200 miles in a single day of riding is a solid effort. To do so back-to-back-to-back over a period of multiple months is physically exhausting.

In addition to exhaustion, it is also a debilitating undertaking. Every part of the body has to be able to cope with the strain of being in a fixed position for periods in excess of 12 hours per day, every day. Leg muscles and tendons bear the brunt of the effort, and it is not uncommon for cyclists to return from this ride carrying multiple injuries. The back and neck are also placed under considerable strain, as are the hands (which have to support the weight of the upper body for days on end). For cyclists to hit their targets in the pursuit of a Guinness World Record, they need to self-remedy while riding through constant discomfort.

Physical exhaustion and injuries simply add to the other formidable obstacle that stands in the way of completing a ride around the world: the mind. For obvious reasons, most cyclists who attempt a circumnavigation of the globe do so on their own. As such, they alone are responsible for dealing with any problems – physical or logistical – and managing themselves through the inevitable difficult periods of the ride. Having the right mindset – and in particular an unwillingness to give up – is therefore essential to success. Cumulative fatigue during the trip simply adds to the difficulty of maintaining a positive mental attitude, with cyclists often struggling to ward off their negative thoughts.

It goes without saying that on a journey around the world, cyclists can experience any number of terrains, weather conditions and even people. Some have talked about being chased by packs of semi-wild dogs, others

of being knocked off their bikes by road trains in the desert, and a few of cycling into perpetual headwinds or cyclones. Because of the nature of the challenge, it is simply impossible to capture all of the possible different conditions faced by those attempting it. Needless to say, though, any circumnavigator has to be prepared to deal with any number of variables that are both beyond their control and often entirely unexpected.

A ride around the world is a tremendous undertaking. For some adventurous souls, it is a journey of rich experiences that can last for many years. For a select few it is, essentially, a race against time. For all who try to complete it, it is an opportunity to see how their bodies and minds respond to the relentless demands of the world's longest bike ride.

Juliana Buhring

I really did just wake up one day and decide to cycle the world. Maybe something was triggered in my head by a friend cycling across Canada. I went online and was looking at the men who had cycled the world and realised that there had never been a woman who had done it for any sort of time. I had never really cycled before so for me it was an endeavour of let's see how far we're going to get.

I thought if I'm going to do the circumnavigation then I might as well do it in a record time. If I don't manage it then okay, but if I do then why not go for it? I guess my point was that anyone could go off and do crazy stuff – it doesn't take an extraordinary person. I wasn't an athlete or anybody.

I had moments a few days in when I thought 'what have I got myself into?' But for me at the same time it was about setting off into the unknown and going on an adventure. At that moment it was what I needed to do and that's what I did.

Everyone was telling me that I was going the wrong way because I went the opposite direction to most people. I went east to west, which meant that about 70% of the way there was a lot of headwinds.

I had a really rough time in India. I got really ill and had diarrhoea, and every time I stopped I was mobbed by huge groups of staring men, which was intimidating. Then a cyclone hit the south coast so I pedalled through that for four days. I was so relieved when I left.

The roughest part was the last couple of weeks when I was so close to the finish line. I was physically and mentally completely done, and when I entered Italy there was a cold snap and the temperature dropped to -9°C and I got really bad frostbite. I was struggling just to stay warm, let alone cycle 200km per day. At that point, it's really all in the mind. When the mind gives up, the rest of the body will collapse. That was my lowest point because my mind was ready to finish. What I learnt from that is that as long as you decide to keep going – even if your body should give out – you can keep going indefinitely if your brain isn't ready to quit.

When you get to those difficult moments like cycling through a cyclone or out-running a pack of dogs, you get this incredible high afterwards. You feel so powerful as a human being. Then you realise you have to hit the lows to get the highs. You can endure anything after that.

Juliana Buhring circumnavigated the globe in 152 days – a Guinness World Record. For more information, visit: www.julianabuhring.com.

Type Mixed
Date Year-round
Distance minimum 24,901 miles
(40,075km)
Main challenges Time, injury, conditions

Competitors say
❝*This was never going to be anything other than a multi-year journey with 16 fairly major expeditions back to back.*❞
Jason Lewis

A Human-Powered Circumnavigation of the Globe

Circumnavigating the globe in any way is a formidable challenge. Doing so under the pre-requisite of human power alone simply adds another layer of complexity to it. It is to combine a number of the hardest physical challenges on earth into a single, epic expedition.

right Lewis' journey 'was never going to be anything other than a multi-year journey with 16 fairly major expeditions back-to-back'
below When Jason Lewis set out to rollerblade across the USA he was new to the sport. By the time he had finished he was rather good...

Although there is no strict definition of what constitutes a circumnavigation of the globe, it is generally agreed that any individual or team looking to do so must cover a minimum of 24,901 miles (40,075km) – the distance around the equator. To ensure that this distance is travelled, an attempt should pass through one pair of antipodal points – two places on the globe that are diametrically opposite to one another. In so doing, the expedition is forced to visit both the Northern and Southern hemispheres.

The physical component of any human-powered circumnavigation is itself something of a paradox: simple to define but difficult to execute. On land, human power constitutes anything from walking to cycling and even rollerblading. On the water, individuals can row, swim or use a pedal boat if they choose. In short, they can employ any means of travel they choose, as long as they – and they alone – are responsible for their propulsion (for the purposes of clarity, a sail boat is not a legitimate means of travel in this challenge).

Needless to say, a human-powered circumnavigation of the globe is an enormous physical, mental and logistical undertaking. Not only does it

take those who attempt it many years to complete, but also pits them against some of the most inhospitable – and dangerous – places on the planet.

The individuals determine the starting location of any attempt themselves. However, regardless of where they begin their journey, they will at some point be forced to cross the two largest bodies of water in the world – the Pacific and Atlantic Oceans. The former, in particular, is the toughest oceanic crossing, regardless of the means by which the individual or teams choose to attempt it. Of the two

above Jason Lewis completed his epic journey over the course of 13 years

recognised human-powered circumnavigations completed so far, Jason Lewis became the first person to pedal across the Pacific (from San Francisco, USA, to Cairns, Australia) in his hybrid pedal boat, the Moksha. Ergan Eruç, meanwhile, spent 312 days rowing the ocean – the longest time spent solo at sea – during his 9,072 mile (16,802km) crossing from Bodega Bay (California, USA) to Papua New Guinea.

Eruç's circumnavigation is also notable because he became the first person to have rowed across the Pacific (9,072 miles/16,802km), Indian (5,086 miles/9,421km) and Atlantic (5,465 miles/10,121km) Oceans.

Crossing oceans of any size in human-powered craft is a formidable and dangerous undertaking. As well as freak waves and violent storms that can easily capsize or damage a boat, expeditions travel through areas of water where currents can make forward progress nigh on impossible. Jason Lewis spent 2.5 weeks alone pedalling

against the infamous Pacific doldrums before he was able to battle his way into the southern hemisphere. What's more, nutrition and hydration is difficult to manage during lengthy expeditions on these stretches of water, and salt sores are an inevitable and uncomfortable ailment.

On land, things aren't necessarily much easier. While running, cycling or rollerblading are relatively straightforward pursuits, doing so over many thousands of miles are challenges worthy of this book in their own right. What's more, they can be just as dangerous as time spent at sea. During his expedition, Jason Lewis was detained on suspicion of espionage in Northern Africa, and had both his legs broken after being hit by a car during a record-breaking rollerblade crossing of North America.

As well as the physical and mental challenges involved with a human-powered circumnavigation of the world, there is the logistical element to consider. This expedition is not cheap, and fundraising efforts often add long periods of time to the challenge.

Those fundraising efforts explain why Expedition 360, which saw Jason Lewis become the first person to achieve the circumnavigation, took 13 years 2 months 23 days 11 hours (4,833 days and 11 hours) to cover the 46,505 miles (74,408km). Lewis not only spent that time travelling and fundraising, but also formed a charity out of it. Ergan Eruç became the first person to complete the circumnavigation solo in 2012 (Lewis had companions on various stretches of his expedition), covering 41,196 miles (66,299km) in five years and eleven days (1,026 days of travel).

A human-powered circumnavigation of the globe combines some of the world's toughest physical challenges into one epic expedition. Any individual that is able to complete it will not only have shown great resilience and persistence, but can also rest assured that there are few – if any – challenges greater on the face of this earth.

Jason Lewis

All the independent components of the journey had all effectively been done before, but it seemed like a fairly obvious thing to link those up together into one continuous loop around the planet.

This journey differs to a lot of others. This was never going to be anything other than a multi-year journey with 16 fairly major expeditions back-to-back without coming home. If you're doing something that lasts three or four months, it's easier to save the money for something like that, or convince a marketing manager to stump up the money because they will see the return on investment. This was never going to be less than four years, and that immediately made it difficult to raise the money. One day I worked out that for every hour of travel time, it took three hours to raise money for that hour.

Rollerblading across the US was hardest physically – partly because I was an amateur when I left Miami. It was the summer; I left Miami in June, which is the worst month in the Deep South. And inline skating is harder work than biking – 30-40 miles would be a decent day. On water, kayaking was the hardest. I could pedal the boat 50–60 miles fairly easily. But with paddling the kayak, again 25 miles would be a decent day.

The Pacific was challenging. The trick to these big expanses of water is to break them up. And the nice thing about the Pacific is that you have islands like Hawaii, the Solomon Islands to do that. The psychological prospect of setting off with 10,000 miles of water to cross – that's a fairly intimidating thing to take on. But if you know there is an island 2,500 miles away, that makes it more tolerable.

The hardest thing I found pedalling across the Pacific was being stuck in the middle of the Equatorial counter-current, also known as the doldrums. It's a 400 mile stretch of water just north of the Equator, and the water is running back eastwards towards Central America. You just don't know how long you're going to be stuck in it for. I was fortunate because I was only there for two and a half weeks. Even that was hell, pedalling effectively on the spot. When you're not getting anywhere it's very hard to maintain your morale because nothing changes. It's flat calm and there's no wind. You're like a hamster on a wheel looking at a blank wall. I was lucky because after a few weeks I was able to find one of these worm holes and get into the southern hemisphere. I had a friend who was rowing across the Pacific and he was stuck in it for months.

After most long journeys like these you have an inevitable slump. I knew that was coming because I would experience it at the end of every individual leg. I was prepared for that. There was of course a tremendous sense of accomplishment – and peace. I remember pedalling up the River Thames to the Greenwich Meridian Line and it was the only day in the entire expedition that I can remember being calm and collected, not worried about logistics and things. I found afterwards it was difficult to re-assimilate back into society.

Now I feel complete. I feel like I found the answers that I was looking for. And that I have pushed myself far and beyond – I know what my limits are now. I don't need to go and do another extended expedition to prove something.

Jason Lewis is an explorer and sustainability campaigner. He was the first person to circumnavigate the globe by human power alone. For more information, visit: www.jasonexplorer.com.

Index

Acknowledgements

The concept was simple: write a book about the world's most awe-inspiring physical challenges. The execution ... well, there were a few road bumps along the way.

To be able to get to this point there are a lot of people that I need to say thank you to.

First and foremost, I would like to thank the following athletes (and their representatives) for taking the time to talk with me to share their remarkable stories and experiences. I apologise if at any time you felt chased, harassed or generally harangued. In no particular order other than alphabetical, these athletes are:

Frankie Andreu, Michael Asher, Ram Barkai, Lisa Smith-Batchen, Felix Baumgartner, Peter Bray, Eugene Buchanan, Juliana Buhring, Christine Jensen Burke, Tommy Caldwell, Goran Čolak, Andrew Cotton, Jeremy Curl, Mick Dawson, Cyril Depres, Orlando Duque, John Fegyveresi, Anne-Marie Flammersfeld, Will Gadd, Rob Greenwood, Vicky Griffiths, Tim Hewitt, Alan Hinkes, Dean Karnazes, Wayne Kurtz, Nigel Lamb, Eric Larsen, Benoît Lecomte, Martin Letzter, Jason Lewis, Chloë McCardell, Janette Murray-Wakelin, Freddy Nock, Herbert Nitsch, Børge Ousland, Mark Pattinson, Jay Petervary, Robert Pollhammer, Lara Prior-Palmer, Nicki Rehn, Karl Shields, William Sichel, Cecilie Skog, Ed Stafford, Rosie Swale-Pope, Stephen Roche, Eric Spoto, Petar Stoychev, Borut Strel, Martin Strel, Björn Suneson, Heather Swan, Jean Luc Van Den Heede, Ed Viesturs, Ryan Waters, Jack White, Charlie Wittmack, Levison Wood and Marco Xausa.

I would also like to thank Charlotte, Sarah and Nick at Bloomsbury for their help, patience and direction with this project.

To my friends, thank you for the support (as always). To my family, thank you for putting up with the endless hours of me thinking and talking about this book. I would not be able to do any of this without you. And finally, Eva. You are incredibly patient, wonderfully supportive, and my unfailing motivation. This book is as much yours as it is mine and I owe you a thousand thanks for holding my hand through every word that was written.

Picture Credits

pp.1, 2-3 © Getty Images ■ pp.4-5, 8-9 © 4 Deserts Race Series/www.4deserts.com ■ pp.6-7 © Martin Letzter/se7ensummits.com ■ **A Jump from the Edge of Space** © Getty Images p.13 ■ **Climb the Eight-Thousanders** © Getty Images, pp. 15, 16 ■ **High Altitude Wingsuit Flying** © Getty Images, pp. 18–20 ■ **Climb K2** © Christine Jensen Burke, pp. 22 and 23; © Lapka Sherpa, p.23 ■ **Climb Helmcken Falls Spray Cave** © Christian Pondella/Red Bull Content Pool, pp. 25, 26, 27 and 29 ■ **Walk the High Wire** © Getty Images, pp. 30–1 ■ **Climb the North Face of the Eiger** © Press Association Images, p.33; © Getty Images p.34 ■ **Ski down Mount Everest** © Martin Letzer/se7ensummits.com, pp. 36–8 ■ **Climbing Dawn Wall El Capitan** © Press Association Images, p.39; © Getty Images, p.41 ■ **The Tour De France** © Getty Images, pp. 44–6 ■ **The Deepest Freedive** © Herbert Nitsch, pp. 47–49 ■ **Red Bull Air Race** © Andreas Schaad/Red Bull Content Pool, p.51; © Predrag Vuckovic/Red Bull Content Pool, p.52, © Joerg Mitter/Red Bull Content Pool, p.53; © Predrag Vuckovic/Red Bull Content Pool, p.54; © Samo Vidic/Red Bull Content Pool, p.55 ■ **Maratón Acuático Internacional Hernandárias-Paraná** © Getty Images, p.51 ■ **Win the Triple Crown of Cycling** © Getty Images, pp. 60–1 ■ **Cliff Diving** © Balazs Gardi/Red Bull Content Pool, p.62; © Romina Amato/Red Bull Content Pool, p.63; © Dean Treml/Red Bull Content Pool, p.64; © Romina Amato/Red Bull Content Pool, p.65 ■ **Triple Deca Ironman** © Jozef Kubica, pp. 68–9 ■ **Self Transcendence 3100-mile race** © Jowan Gauthier, pp. 71–2 ■ **Yukon Arctic Ultra** © Montane – Martin Hartley, pp. 74–7 ■ **Race Across America** © Alexander Karelly, pp.78–9 ■ **The Tour Divide** © Eddie Clark, pp. 81–2 ■ **4 Deserts Grand Slam** © 4 Deserts Race Series/www.4deserts.com, pp. 84–5, 87 ■ **The Dakar Rally** © Getty Images, pp. 88–9, 90, 91 ■ **The Barkley Marathons** © Getty Images, pp. 92–4 ■ **Mongol Derby** © The Adventurists, pp. 96–9 ■ **Tor des Geants** © Enrico Romanzi, p.100; © Cristophe Le Saux, p.101; © Courthoud PH, p.102 ■ **Lift Massive Weights** © Getty Images, p.104–5 ■ **The Iditarod Trail Invitational** © Andy Heading, p.107-108 ■ **Surf the World's Biggest Wave** © Getty Images, pp. 112–13 ■ **Kayak Across the Atlantic** © Press Association Images, pp. 115, 117 ■ **Amazon swim** © Strel Swimming, pp. 118–20 ■ **Static Apnoea** © Getty Images, pp. 121–2 ■ **Ice Swimming** © Ram Barkai, p.124 and Getty Images, p.125 ■ **Kayak the Lower Bashkaus Gorge** © the addidas Sickline Team, pp. 127-9 ■ **Swim Across the Atlantic** © Getty Images, pp. 130–2 ■ **Row across the Pacific** © Mick Dawson, pp. 133–6 ■ **Swim the Florida Straits** © Getty Images, pp. 138–9 ■ **Trek to the North Pole** © Eric Larsen, pp. 142–5 ■ **Walk the Length of the Nile** © Levison Wood and Tom McShane, p.147 ■ **Multi-day, non-stop run** © Getty Images, pp.149–150 ■ **Trek Across the Sahara** © Getty Images, pp. 152–4 ■ **Run Across America** © Björn Suneson, pp. 156, 158 ■ **Trek Solo Across Antarctica** © Berge Ousland, p.160–1 ■ **Run around Australia** © Janette Murray-Wakelin, pp.163–4 ■ **Badwater Quad** © Getty Images, p.166, © Vincent M. Antunez, pp. 167–8 ■ **Walk the Length of the Amazon** © Getty Images, pp. 169–70 ■ **The Explorers' Grand Slam** © Getty Images, pp. 175–6 ■ **Westerly Solo Sail Around the World** © Getty Images, pp. 178–80 ■ **A Pedestrian Circumnavigation of the World** © Getty Images, pp. 181–3 ■ **Cycling around the world** © Juliana Buhring, pp. 184-5; © EddieClarkMedia/InspiredToRide.it, p.186 ■ **Human powered circumnavigation of the globe** © Jason Lewis, p.187, © Getty Images, p.188